MAKING ECONOMIC POLICY

Kenneth I. Juster
Simon Lazarus

MAKING ECONOMIC POLICY

An Assessment of the National Economic Council

BROOKINGS INSTITUTION PRESS
Washington, D.C.

Library of Congress Cataloging-in-Publication data
Juster, Kenneth I.
    Making economic policy: an assessment of the National Economic Council / Kenneth
    I. Juster, Simon Lazarus.
        p.   cm.
    Includes bibliographical references.
    ISBN 0-8157-4775-6 (pbk. : alk. paper)
    1. United States—Economic policy—Decision making.
    2. Administrative agencies—United States—History—20th century.
    3. Presidents—United States—History—20th century.   I. Lazarus,
    Simon.   II. Title.
    HC106.J87   1997
    338.973—dc21   96-45915
                                                               CIP

9 8 7 6 5 4 3 2 1

The paper used in this publication meets the minimum requirements of the American
National Standard for Information Sciences—Permanence of Paper for Printed
Library Materials, ANSI Z39.48-1984.

Set in Times Roman and Futura

Composition by Cynthia Stock
Silver Spring, Maryland

Printed by Kirby Lithographic
Arlington, Virginia

THE BROOKINGS INSTITUTION

The Brookings Institution is an independent organization devoted to nonpartisan research, education, and publication in economics, government, foreign policy, and the social sciences generally. Its principal purposes are to aid in the development of sound public policies and to promote public understanding of issues of national importance.

The Institution was founded on December 8, 1927, to merge the activities of the Institute for Government Research, founded in 1916, the Institute of Economics, founded in 1922, and the Robert Brookings Graduate School of Economics and Government, founded in 1924.

The Board of Trustees is responsible for the general administration of the Institution, while the immediate direction of the policies, program, and staff is vested in the President, assisted by an advisory committee of the officers and staff. The by-laws of the Institution state: "It is the function of the Trustees to make possible the conduct of scientific research, and publication, under the most favorable conditions, and to safeguard the independence of the research staff in the pursuit of their studies and in the publication of the results of such studies. It is not a part of their function to determine, control, or influence the conduct of particular investigations or the conclusions reached."

The President bears final responsibility for the decision to publish a manuscript as a Brookings book. In reaching his judgment on the competence, accuracy, and objectivity of each study, the President is advised by the director of the appropriate research program and weighs the views of a panel of expert outside readers who report to him in confidence on the quality of the work. Publication of a work signifies that it is deemed a competent treatment worthy of public consideration but does not imply endorsement of conclusions or recommendations.

The Institution maintains its position of neutrality on issues of public policy in order to safeguard the intellectual freedom of the staff. Hence interpretations or conclusions in Brookings publications should be understood to be solely those of the authors and should not be attributed to the Institution, to its trustees, officers, or other staff members, or to the organizations that support its research.

Foreword

Every administration establishes a mechanism for making and coordinating economic policy. The particular systems employed in each administration have all been aimed at developing economic policies consistent with the president's priorities.

In 1993, President Clinton created a National Economic Council (NEC) to integrate and coordinate his administration's economic policies. The NEC may not have been a radical departure from the past, but it clearly was a new approach, located in the White House, with a broad charter covering both international and domestic economic policy and a top-level manager, the assistant to the president for economic policy.

The NEC differed enough from its predecessors and was apparently successful enough to warrant a special comparative analysis and evaluation. To ensure that an evaluation be available for the president elected on November 5, 1996, and his advisors, as well as for scholars generally, the Brookings Institution commissioned Kenneth I. Juster and Simon Lazarus, whose policymaking experience spans Republican and Democratic administrations, to produce *Making Economic Policy: An Assessment of the National Economic Council.*

Lazarus and Juster confirmed that the NEC represents a constructive evolution in the development and coordination of economic policy in the executive branch. They conclude that the NEC should be maintained and used broadly, and they offer a wide array of recommendations for its improvement that should be a valuable guide to President Clinton in his second term and to future presidents. Their work may be as important to the development of the NEC as the reports of the Cuomo commission and the Carnegie Endowment for International Peace/Institute for International Economics were to its creation.

In their search for information about the NEC and its predecessors, Juster and Lazarus conducted more than sixty detailed, confidential interviews with key personnel representing the Clinton administration and seven predecessor administrations. The authors' guarantee of confidentiality will, of course, be maintained. Brookings is extremely grateful to these very busy men and women, who gave generously of their valuable time to assist in this evaluation.

The Brookings Institution also owes its thanks to the special group of advisors listed on the next page, whose wise counsel helped to guide the work of the authors. These advisors provided helpful insights, but it must be noted that *Making Economic Policy* is exclusively the work of Simon Lazarus and Kenneth Juster.

We commend their study to all who are interested in the formulation of American economic policy.

WILLIAM E. FRENZEL
LEWIS KADEN

Washington, D.C.
November 1996

Steering Committee

The Interviewees

Roger C. Altman

John Angell

James A. Baker III

William E. Barreda

Charlene Barshefsky

Lloyd Bentsen

Samuel R. Berger

William J. Burns

George H. W. Bush

Warren Christopher

Richard N. Cooper

W. Bowman Cutter

Charles H. Dallara

Kenneth W. Dam

Richard G. Darman

Paul Dimond

Lawrence S. Eagleburger

Stuart E. Eizenstat

James H. Fall

Robert C. Fauver

Gerald R. Ford

William A. Galston

Joshua Gotbaum

Patrick Griffin

Carla A. Hills

Michael Kantor

Julius L. Katz

Lawrence F. Katz

Robert M. Kimmitt

Ronald A. Klain

Sandra Kristoff

Robert D. Kyle

Alan P. Larson

Deborah Lehr

Jacob Joseph Lew

Sylvia Mathews

Thomas F. McLarty III

Eric D. K. Melby

David C. Mulford

Alicia H. Munnell

Thomas O'Donnell

Howard G. Paster

Bruce Reed

Robert B. Reich

Alice M. Rivlin

Dorothy Robyn

Robert E. Rubin

Lee M. Sands

Charles L. Schultze

Susan C. Schwab

Brent Scowcroft

Ellen Seidman

L. William Seidman

Jeffrey R. Shafer

Ira S. Shapiro

George P. Shultz

Gene Sperling

Joan E. Spero

George R. Stephanopoulos

Joseph E. Stiglitz

Lawrence H. Summers

Daniel K. Tarullo

Laura D'Andrea Tyson

Olin L. Wethington

Robert B. Zoellick

The Authors

Kenneth I. Juster is a partner in the law firm of Arnold & Porter, where his practice involves international law, general litigation, and corporate counseling. He served as the counselor (acting) of the U.S. Department of State from August 1992 to January 1993, and as the deputy and senior adviser to Deputy Secretary of State Lawrence S. Eagleburger from August 1989 to August 1992. He also worked at the National Security Council in 1978. Mr. Juster holds a J.D. from the Harvard Law School, a master in public policy from the John F. Kennedy School of Government at Harvard University, and an A.B. from Harvard College.

Simon Lazarus is a partner in the law firm of Powell, Goldstein, Frazer & Murphy, where his practice involves public policy advocacy, administrative law, and antitrust. He served as an associate director of the White House Domestic Policy Staff from 1977 to 1981. Mr. Lazarus holds an LL.B. from the Yale Law School, a master in urban studies from Yale University, and an A.B. from Harvard College.

The authors thank Frances W. Davis, Harold P. Luks, Ronald E. Minsk, Nancy L. Perkins, and Carmelita A. San Jose for their assistance in the preparation of this report.

Contents

Executive Summary

Introduction

- One of the most noted first steps of the Clinton administration was creation of a National Economic Council (NEC) located in the White House.
- The NEC was inspired, in part, by recommendations made by two commissions in 1992, one created by New York Governor Mario Cuomo (which included both Robert E. Rubin and Laura D'Andrea Tyson, the two successive NEC advisors to date) and the other assembled jointly by the Carnegie Endowment for International Peace and the Institute for International Economics. In the view of the latter commission, establishing a White House–based coordinating mechanism such as the NEC represented an "essential" post–cold war reorganization of government to shift resources "away from national security, as traditionally defined, toward the broader problems of making America competitive in a fiercely competitive world."
- In creating the NEC, the Clinton transition planners also borrowed from examples set by previous administrations, which

had established mechanisms with similar elements for coordinating economic policy.

- For the Clinton White House, the establishment of the NEC sent a political message to its administration that it would explicitly use policy machinery to make economics a priority—a message previously conveyed by a famous sign in the Clinton campaign office: "It's the economy, stupid."

- This report was undertaken to address whether the NEC experiment was a good idea. Is it working? Does it help the president achieve his goals in the way its architects expected? Where has it fallen short? What does the NEC experience, as well as the experiences of predecessor administrations, tell a new administration about how to structure the president's management of economic policy? Should the NEC be codified by statute?

- To examine these and related questions, we interviewed over sixty officials in the Clinton administration and in predecessor administrations, including two former presidents.

  - In conducting and evaluating the results of these interviews, our focus has been on the interests of the president—practical advice on what decision structures and procedures best serve the president.

  - The records of our interviews comprise a valuable trove of observations and perspectives on which to base conclusions and recommendations. We have not been in a position, however, to examine the NEC's documentary record, nor to question all participants in key events. Accordingly, this report is not intended to be viewed as a definitive historical account.

Principal Conclusions

- Overall, the NEC, when utilized, has served President Clinton and his administration well. By and large, those major economic initiatives that were thoroughly vetted through the NEC (or jointly with other coordinating bodies such as the National Security Council) held up relatively well after they were announced or submitted to Congress.

- The most prominent example of NEC coordination was its first undertaking: the development of the five-year deficit reduction package, including a proposed budget for fiscal year 1994 containing numerous new programs and revisions of existing programs, as well as a $16 billion economic stimulus package, submitted to Congress on February 17, 1993.
  - This NEC-led process required the president and his key advisors to prioritize the proposals championed during his campaign, subject them to the discipline of the budget process, and submit a legislative package to Congress less than a month after they moved into their new offices.
  - In this process, the administration made a fundamental decision: to make long-term deficit reduction and low interest rates a central strategic priority and, simultaneously, to defer the campaign's promise of "middle class tax cuts" and reduce substantially funds for "public investment" in infrastructure and human capital (another major campaign commitment).
  - Although this trade-off among priorities was difficult for the president, as well as for key members of the administration and important constituencies, the NEC process provided all players with the collective opportunity to identify the options, grasp their consequences, press individual views, and ultimately accept and support the president's decisions.
- In view of the fact that the budget plan encountered serious unanticipated difficulties after reaching Capitol Hill, including rejection of the economic stimulus package, before the overall plan passed by razor-thin margins, it appears that the NEC process may not have given adequate attention to the politics of the issues considered. But overall, especially given the compressed time frame, the process of developing this initial budget plan served the president well.
- Other examples of effective NEC coordination with positive payoff for the president are the decisions to press for enactment of legislation implementing the North American Free Trade Agreement (NAFTA) (including the labor and environmental side agreements) and legislation implementing the Uruguay Round agreement; the development of a framework for negotia-

tions designed to further open Japanese markets; the June 1995 proposal for phasing in a balanced budget by the year 2002; the "Middle Class Bill of Rights" package of targeted tax deductions and credits announced in December 1994; and the series of smaller policy initiatives, including tax and other proposals, announced during the second and third quarters of 1996.

- In contrast, there were significant economic initiatives that were not subjected to thorough and inclusive coordination and that were widely regarded as policy failures.

  - Although the 1994 health care reform plan failed for several reasons, one of the basic problems, according to virtually every official with whom we spoke, was the lack of a meaningful effort to solicit or take seriously the views of key agencies and officials, including the principal members of the NEC, during the development of the plan.

  - Many also view the 1993 decision to condition most-favored-nation (MFN) treatment for China on "significant progress" on human rights—again, a decision in which the NEC was not significantly involved—as a key foreign policy failure.

- The NEC is still, as one senior Clinton official observed, "a work in progress," and important aspects of its operations, as well as how other elements of the administration relate to and interact with the NEC, could be strengthened. As another official observed, the NEC functioned "in different ways in different areas at different times." More specifically:

  - The NEC was (when used) highly successful in effecting coordination and harmony at the top, among its "principals"—cabinet members and senior officials in the Executive Office of the President—in vetting and "debugging" policy proposals, exposing the president to all sides of controversial issues, minimizing turf competition, and ultimately retaining support for the president's decisions among those whose advice he did not follow.

  - The NEC took the lead as "keeper of the flame"—ensuring that individual initiatives conformed to the president's policy and political priorities (for example, by insisting that new policy proposals were "paid for" with off-setting spending cuts or revenue generation)—and in communicating the administration's positions, economic accomplishments, and themes.

- The NEC gave international trade policy a high profile and gave increased clout to economic considerations on selected foreign policy issues other than trade. There is, however, room for further progress on this front, both within the NEC itself and between the NEC and other involved entities, including the National Security Council (NSC).

- The administration's record was uneven in giving economics broader impact on domestic policymaking and in implementing the "public investment" approach to social programs emphasized by the 1992 Clinton campaign.

- The NEC has been more structured in its coordination of international economic issues (primarily trade policy) than it has been on domestic issues, in part because of the established group of agencies involved in such international matters. The NEC deputy advisor now chairs weekly deputies' meetings on international economic issues, which are generally regarded as a successful routine for identifying and resolving specific issues, or presenting them for resolution at higher levels.

- The NEC, especially on domestic issues, does not appear to have created a consistently effective decision management structure below the deputy level, integrated with its own top-level staff (including deliberations of the deputies and the principals) or with interagency working group processes.

- The NEC's comparatively informal, ad hoc operational style, which helped at the outset to create a collegial environment, also has entailed drawbacks, according to a number of Clinton administration officials: inefficiency in the form of long and sometimes unfocused meetings with unclear outcomes, an absence of predictable or consistent procedures (except for the recent weekly meetings among deputies), and a failure of the NEC to establish strategic priorities on a systematic basis.

- In sum, the NEC has worked well as a device for enabling the senior members of the Clinton economic team to stay together, refine options and recommendations for the president, and magnify their collective influence on a broad spectrum of issue-areas and administration actions. But this is a fragile experiment.

- As yet, the NEC appears to have achieved relatively little institutionalization: regularity of internal procedures from issue to issue, continuity over time in managing and monitoring decisionmaking processes, and a sense of permanence to the NEC structure despite changes within its staff.

- The NEC has not created a *modus operandi* that has enduring value apart from the particular individuals engaged in the process at a given point in time.

Upcoming Agenda

- The agenda facing the new administration will include challenging, cross-cutting issues with significant economic content, ripe for the attention of an NEC.

  - On the domestic side, all priorities will have to be squared with the long-term budget commitments made in June 1995. Specific challenges will include:

    (i)   revamping the major entitlement programs (medicare, medicaid, and social security) to accommodate demographic trends in the twenty-first century;

    (ii) implementing welfare reform (possibly determining changes to propose) with a credible approach to prepare welfare recipients for the job market and provide jobs once eligibility has expired;

    (iii) considering additional education and training initiatives; and

    (iv) developing incremental health care reform legislation.

  - On the international side, the administration will face a range of challenges to maintain a political environment compatible with U.S. engagement and leadership in the world, including:

    (i)   sustaining support for the continued liberalization of international trade, by obtaining "fast track" negotiating authority and moving forward on regional free trade arrangements;

(ii)   attempting to manage the smooth integration into the world economy of China, Russia, and emerging regional powers such as India and Brazil (which will include in some cases the issue of accession to the World Trade Organization);

(iii) addressing the financial and political ramifications of European movement toward monetary union (a likely subject for discussion at the 1997 G-7 summit to be held in Denver, Colorado); and

(iv)   developing internationally effective and domestically sustainable policies on the use of economic sanctions, export controls, and other measures to try to curb terrorism and the proliferation of weapons of mass destruction.

- Whether this is in fact the president's agenda of strategic priorities, he must decide promptly, at the outset of his administration, where he wants to try to make his mark, and to organize his staff accordingly. Fundamental decisions regarding the president's agenda should inform structural decisions about the jurisdiction and organization of entities that coordinate policy development.

Principal Recommendations

On the basis of these observations, we offer the following principal recommendations:

1. Given the bipartisan consensus that the global position of the U.S. economy remains a priority concern, and in light of the agenda of economic issues facing the new president, the administration should retain the NEC with substantially its current mission.

   - From a president's perspective, coordination generally works best when the process is managed by a senior White House aide.
   - The mission of the White House coordinator should be to serve as honest broker, advisor, and "keeper of the flame."

2. Obvious though it seems, it is worth underscoring the importance of picking an economic team and White House senior staff

as a unit, with multiple and complementary skills and with mutually accepted roles.

3. Immediately after the election, the NEC should undertake a systematic process for setting strategic economic priorities and goals for the coming year.

    •   The NEC, working with and drawing on the resources of other entities as appropriate, should have responsibility to identify major domestic and international economic issues, recommend presidential priorities, and provide a coherent framework for approaching these issues.

    •   The process should produce well-defined goals and specific assignments of responsibility for achieving them.

    •   This exercise of setting of strategic economic priorities for the president should be repeated annually.

4. The NEC, again working with and drawing on the resources of others as appropriate, should ensure that the administration is aware of longer-term economic trends, both domestically and internationally, and considers alternative policy strategies and scenarios for addressing those trends.

5. The new administration should take the next steps necessary to give economics more consistent impact in foreign policymaking. It should, for example:

    •   Improve coordination between the NEC and the NSC by, among other things:

        (i)   continuing the precedent set in the first Clinton administration of utilizing a joint NEC/NSC international economics staff, and of ensuring that either the NSC advisor or the NSC deputy has a familiarity with and interest in economic matters;

        (ii)   enhancing NSC economic, commercial, and financial capabilities in regional directorates (where much of the integration of foreign policy occurs);

        (iii)   ensuring consistent and timely inclusion of NEC staff in the development of NSC initiatives with significant economic dimensions; and

        (iv)   having the NSC secretariat work closely with a newly created, three-person NEC secretariat to share briefing papers and other important background material, ensure clearance by the NEC on all NSC papers that have economic components or implications, and ensure that the meetings of deputies and principals generally conclude with written instructions that can be circulated to appropriate agencies for implementation.

- Revitalize the role of the interagency Trade Policy Review Group (TPRG), which has been successfully used in previous administrations, to resolve "second-tier" issues that do not merit the attention of the NEC deputies and to provide improved preparatory work for those issues considered by the deputies or the principals.

6. The new administration should ensure consistent NEC coordination and integration with the apparatus for domestic policy management, so that major domestic issues with economic dimensions, such as entitlement reform, health care and welfare reform, environmental protection, and regulatory policy, receive meaningful NEC attention.

- The president and his key advisors can determine on a case-by-case basis whether the NEC's role should be one of coordinator, joint coordinator, or participant in a process managed by another entity.
- On the basis of decisions about the administration's strategic agenda and priorities, and the NEC's role with respect to each of the priority issues, the NEC should make adjustments in the subject-matter areas covered by its staff.
- Although it is beyond the scope of this report to make recommendations concerning the organization of White House domestic policy management, many officials with whom we spoke felt that NEC participation in domestic policymaking would probably be more effective if responsibility for coordinating domestic policy issues were more clearly demarcated than was the case during the first Clinton term.

7. The new administration should take steps to institutionalize the NEC and enable it to make more effective use of its staff. The administration should, among other things:

- Ensure that NEC staff immediately below the deputy level (currently bearing the title "special assistant to the president for economic policy") possess sufficient stature and are delegated sufficient authority to take a leadership role in harnessing agency expertise and resources to coordinate significant economic issues.

- Impose no artificial constraints (up or down) on the size of the NEC staff: staff size, especially at the special assistant level, should reflect the priorities set by, and match the policy development needs of, the new administration.

- Detail some career civil servants from the departments and agencies to the NEC staff to add continuity and "institutional memory" to NEC activities and help institutionalize the NEC process.

- Ensure that the NEC advisor and deputies consistently provide guidance to the staff regarding their priorities, so that the staff are better able to monitor and stimulate interagency activities; inform NEC superiors (and through them the president) of ongoing decision processes and likely results if the president does not intervene (to give him the chance to do so); and, for issues that merit elevation, arrange to efficiently bring them to the NEC deputies or principals (or other channels to the president).

8. It is premature to codify the NEC structure by statute. Although the NEC has worked relatively well for the Clinton administration, other administrations have used different coordinating structures—some quite successfully—and a president should retain the flexibility to organize his administration in a manner that is most compatible with his personal style and policy objectives. The next step, as noted above, is to strengthen and begin to institutionalize the NEC processes, not try to freeze the NEC structure in statute.

1

Profile of the National Economic Council

Origins of the Concept

- When first put forward by candidate Bill Clinton during the 1992 presidential campaign, the concept of creating a White House economic policy council was cast as a means of strengthening the capacity of the government to promote U.S. economic and commercial interests abroad and enhancing the competitiveness of the U.S. economy.
  - In his June 1992 compendium of campaign policy proposals entitled "Putting People First," Clinton declared his intent to "create an Economic Security Council, similar in status to the National Security Council, with responsibility for coordinating America's international economic policy."
  - Following the publication of "Putting People First," Clinton mentioned the concept only sparingly during the campaign. In an August 1992 speech before the World Affairs Council in Los Angeles, Clinton promised to form an "economic security council similar to the National Security Council

and change the State Department's culture so that economics is no longer a poor cousin to old school diplomacy."

- At the time of the Clinton campaign, the concept of a strong White House economic coordinating council had a degree of currency among the community of close observers of federal policymaking. These observers perceived an important need to upgrade attention to economic concerns in order to promote American competitiveness abroad.

  - In 1992, the Carnegie Endowment for International Peace and the Institute for International Economics (IIE) sponsored a "Commission on Government Renewal," composed of approximately thirty individuals with records of high-level government service. This group published a report prominently recommending the creation of a White House–based economic council for coordinating all economic policy, both domestic and international.

  - The Carnegie/IIE commission stated that "the combination of Cold War victory and deep economic difficulties allows— and indeed, demands—a shift of priority and resources away from national security, as traditionally defined, toward the broader problems of making America competitive in a fiercely competitive world."

  - Addressing the new president, the commission further stated that "the Economic Council and its staff would be your instrument for assuring that economic policy gets attention equal to traditional national security, working extremely closely with the NSC and its staff when international economic issues are under consideration, and with the Domestic Council and its staff on domestic policy matters."

- A similar suggestion was contained in another 1992 report, this one prepared by New York Governor Mario Cuomo's Commission on Competitiveness and Trade. Members of the Cuomo commission discussed their economic security council proposal directly with Clinton at a meeting in the spring of 1992.

Creation of the Council

- During the Clinton transition, as campaign rhetoric about an economic security council took institutional shape, the focus of the council evolved from aggressively promoting U.S. commercial and economic interests abroad to serving as a neutral coordinator of both domestic and international economic issues. In the first instance, the charge was to coordinate a comprehensive federal budget reflecting the president's priorities.

- Ten days after the election, President-elect Clinton selected Robert B. Reich to serve as the director of the economic transition. Reich and others decided that the name "economic security council" sounded too protectionist. A new name was chosen: the National Economic Council.

- Subsequently, at a press conference in Little Rock on December 10, 1992, Clinton announced the appointment of his economic team, including Lloyd Bentsen as his secretary of the treasury and Robert E. Rubin as the assistant to the president for economic affairs, who would head up the National Economic Council. At the press conference, Clinton emphasized that Bentsen would assume the treasury secretary's traditional role as chief economic spokesman for the administration, while the NEC advisor's job would be "very much like General Scowcroft's job on the national security side in [the Bush] Administration . . . to coordinate, to facilitate, and to provide some direction to the deliberations of our economic council."

- Rubin selected two deputies: Gene Sperling, a senior campaign economic policy staffer and Reich's deputy during the transition, and W. Bowman (Bo) Cutter, a senior official of the Office of Management and Budget (OMB) during the Carter administration. Rubin also selected Sylvia Mathews to serve as his special assistant.

  - The group planned the jurisdiction, structure, staffing, and *modus operandi* of the new entity, consulting intensively with other members of the economic team and with former White House policy advisors and other experts.

  - The group also developed with Samuel R. (Sandy) Berger, who had been selected to be deputy national security advisor, the notion of having a joint—"dual-hatted"—international economics staff that would report to both the NEC and the NSC.

- The result of these consultations was a January 1993 memorandum from Rubin to the president-elect setting out in detail the mission and operations of the NEC. The memorandum, the content of which had been agreed to by all members of the economic team, addressed the various facets of the new organization's mission.

- While negotiations over the role of the NEC were in progress, Rubin worked with the prospective members of the coordinating body to develop the new administration's budget.

  - On January 7, 1993, Rubin convened a six-hour meeting in Little Rock with the president-elect to explore budget options. The meeting included presentations by Sperling and several designated cabinet and subcabinet officers: Bentsen (treasury secretary), Leon E. Panetta (OMB director), Laura D'Andrea Tyson (chair of the Council of Economic Advisers), Roger C. Altman (treasury deputy secretary), and Lawrence H. Summers (treasury under secretary for international affairs).

  - Rubin chaired the meeting but made no presentation.

The Charter

- On January 25, 1993, President Clinton signed an executive order formally establishing the NEC (see appendix 1).

  - The executive order stated that "the principal functions of the Council are: (1) to coordinate the economic policy-making process with respect to domestic and international economic issues; (2) to coordinate economic advice to the President; (3) to ensure that economic policy decisions and programs are consistent with the President's stated goals, and to ensure that those goals are being effectively pursued; and (4) to monitor implementation of the President's economic policy agenda."

  - The order further stated that "all executive departments and agencies, whether or not represented on the Council, shall coordinate economic policy through the Council."

  - Finally, it reiterated that the secretary of the treasury would continue to serve as the administration's senior economic official and chief economic spokesman and that the director of OMB and the chair of the Council of Economic Advisers (CEA) would retain their respective budget management and economic policy advisory roles.

- The executive order provided, in effect, a summary of the detailed description of the NEC's jurisdiction, mission, composition, structure, and operations as contained in Rubin's January 1993 memorandum to the president-elect (which Rubin described in a note to NEC members as the NEC "charter" document). Pursuant to the memorandum, the NEC was to coordinate "broad public policy issues affecting the economy (e.g., trade and export policy, defense-conversion policy, infrastructure policy and research and commercial technology policy) . . . [as well as] all aspects of the domestic economic recovery program, including job development strategy, inflation and deficit reduction strategy, investment programs, tax policy and industrial competitiveness strategies . . . [and] such international economic issues as trade, international monetary and financial policy."
- Subsequently, on March 24, 1993, the president distributed a decision directive that reflected much of the detail in the January memorandum from Rubin (see appendix 2).[1]
  - The directive formally established an NEC Principals Committee, consisting of the secretaries of Treasury, Commerce, and Labor, the OMB director, CEA chair, and national security advisor, with other heads of departments or officers

---

1. As provided in the March 24, 1993, directive, the NEC's members were

"the President, the Vice President, the Secretary of State, the Secretary of the Treasury, the Secretary of Agriculture, the Secretary of Commerce, the Secretary of Labor, the Secretary of Housing and Urban Development, the Secretary of Transportation, the Secretary of Energy, the Administrator of the Environmental Protection Agency, the Chair of the Council of Economic Advisers, the Director of the Office of Management and Budget, the United States Trade Representative, the Assistant to the President for Economic Policy, the Assistant to the President for Domestic Policy, the National Security Advisor, and the Assistant to the President for Science and Technology Policy. The heads of other Executive departments and agencies and other senior officials shall be invited to attend meetings of the NEC where appropriate."

Subsequently, the administrator of the Small Business Administration was named a member of the NEC.

invited as needed. The Principals Committee was to serve as "the senior interagency forum for the consideration and integration of policy issues importantly affecting the national economy."

- The directive characterized the Principals Committee, which would be chaired by the NEC advisor in the absence of the president, as "a flexible instrument–a forum available for Cabinet-level officials to meet to discuss and resolve issues not requiring the President's participation."

- The directive also established an NEC Deputies Committee, consisting of representatives, each at the deputy or under secretary level, from the more than fifteen departments or agencies represented on the NEC. The Deputies Committee was designed to serve as "the senior sub-Cabinet interagency forum for consideration of policy issues affecting the national economy."

  - The directive instructed it to "review and monitor the work of the NEC interagency process" and to "focus significant attention on policy implementation."

  - The NEC deputy advisor was charged with calling meetings, preparing agendas, and distributing materials to members before each meeting.

- The directive also authorized a system of interagency working groups to be established at the direction of the deputies.

Overview of the Structure and Operations

- As provided by the March 1993 directive, the NEC operates at three levels: a principals level, a deputies level, and a staff level.

- Much of the NEC's work is conducted at the deputies level. The NEC has two deputy positions, each with distinct functions.

  - Sperling has served as the deputy responsible for budget policy, for communicating the administration's economic policy message, and for ensuring adherence to the president's campaign promises and other priorities.

  - The other NEC deputy—first Bo Cutter and, subsequently, Daniel K. Tarullo—generally has focused on managing nonbudget issues, especially international issues; chairing the interagency deputies committee for coordinating international economic issues; and managing the NEC staff.

- Initially, largely in accordance with the subject-matter areas specified in the January 1993 "charter" memorandum, staff members below the deputy level were assigned to several general issue clusters: international economic policy (with a joint staff serving both the NEC and the NSC); regulatory policy, financial institutions, and community development; energy, environment, and natural resources; research and development, and technology policy; defense conversion and reuse of military bases; and infrastructure and transportation.
- Over the first term of the administration, the NEC staff also assumed responsibility for initiatives involving pension reform, school construction, and—jointly with the Domestic Policy Council (DPC) and, in some instances, OMB—education and training, among other issues.
- In the fall of 1993, the NEC staff numbered approximately twenty-two professionals. By the fall of 1996, it numbered approximately eighteen.
- Each level of the NEC staff appears to have played a somewhat distinct role during the course of the Clinton administration's first term.
- Especially on the domestic side, the staff below the deputy level appear often to have worked on issues different from those that preoccupied the NEC advisor and the deputies.
  - Domestic staff members, according to some with whom we spoke, have operated at times with relatively little guidance from their superiors, particularly the NEC advisor.
  - The international economic policy cluster, however, has worked closely with the NEC deputy overseeing this area, first Cutter and then Tarullo.
- At the deputies level, the NEC appeared to play a relatively consistent role throughout the first four years of the administration, with Sperling focusing on budget and tax policy and Cutter and Tarullo concentrating primarily on international affairs.
- In contrast to the relatively stable roles of the deputies and staff, the role of the NEC advisor and the Principals Committee went through three distinct phases.

- The first phase coincided with the administration's initial year (1993), when the NEC advisor and the principals were at the center of decisionmaking on most of the key issues facing the president.
    - Framing the 1993 budget forced the president and his economics team to sort through the proposals championed during the campaign and to determine which should be included in this first major initiative, which should be dropped, and which should be deferred. The NEC Principals Committee was the vehicle for making these decisions.
    - The Principals Committee also took the lead in shaping policy and strategic choices regarding the trade initiatives that dominated White House attention after passage of the budget plan: the NAFTA and Uruguay Round implementing legislation, negotiations with Japan, and the Asia-Pacific Economic Cooperation (APEC) summit meeting in November 1993.
- In 1994—the second phase—President Clinton made his massive health care reform proposal the overriding priority of the administration.
    - The NEC and its members appear to have played a comparatively peripheral role in the development of this legislation and the attempt to enact it.
    - The principals, however, continued to meet regularly, though less frequently than during the intensive phase of the 1993 budget battle.
- In late 1994 and early 1995—phase three—the policymaking environment in the Clinton White House was transformed.
    - The Republicans' congressional election victory shifted the White House from an offensive mode to a defensive one— from developing its own program agenda to parrying the congressional agenda.
    - Key personnel changes also occurred: Robert Rubin replaced Lloyd Bentsen as treasury secretary, Laura Tyson replaced Rubin as head of the NEC (although after a considerable gap in time before being named), and Leon Panetta moved from OMB to become White House chief of staff.
- Especially after the Republican congressional leadership decided in the spring of 1995 to concentrate on a comprehensive pro-

posal to balance the federal budget by 2002, Panetta's policy role in the White House became central.

- As a former OMB director and former chair of the House Budget Committee, Panetta had unique qualifications to direct the administration's 1995-96 budget battle with Congress.
- Panetta chaired an informal Budget Strategy Group, which included NEC Advisor Tyson and NEC Deputy Sperling, Treasury Secretary Rubin, and OMB Director Alice M. Rivlin, as well as White House political aides George R. Stephanopolous and Patrick Griffin and CEA Chair Joseph E. Stiglitz. Meetings of the Budget Strategy Group generally did not include representatives from Labor or Commerce, who are NEC core members.
- While Tyson and Sperling retained their influence as individuals in the economic inner circle, most officials we interviewed felt that Panetta and the Budget Strategy Group became the institutional center of budget policy and decisions.

- After Panetta became chief of staff, the NEC process was still frequently used for policy development at the principals level, especially with regard to international trade and other major foreign economic policy issues.

2

Alternative Models for Economic Policy Coordination

E very modern administration has developed mechanisms to coordinate economic policymaking. The NEC is only one example of such mechanisms. As suggested throughout this volume, an examination of the alternative structures that have been used in previous administrations is useful in assessing the performance of the NEC and in recommending possible modifications to its processes.

One way of evaluating alternative policymaking structures, as suggested by Roger Porter and others, is to conceptualize these structures within the framework of three principal models: centralized, multiple advocacy, and ad hoc.[2] There are, of course, other ways of conceptualiz-

---

2. See Roger B. Porter, *Presidential Decision Making: The Economic Policy Board* (Cambridge University Press, 1980), pp. 229–52. See also George P. Shultz and Kenneth W. Dam, *Economic Policy beyond the Headlines* (Norton, 1978), pp. 155–78; I. M. Destler, *Making Foreign Economic Policy* (Brookings, 1980), pp. 1–18, 211–28; Ben W. Heineman Jr. and Curtis A. Hessler, *Memorandum for the President: A Strategic Approach to Domestic Affairs in the 1980s* (Random House, 1980), pp. 176–250; James P. Pfiffner, *The President and Economic Policy* (Institute for the Study of Human Issues, 1986), pp. 90–99; and Alexander L. George, "Making Foreign Policy," *American Political Science Review,* vol. 66 (September 1972), pp. 751–85.

ing decisionmaking models; moreover, these models are not mutually exclusive. As indicated below, most of the recent administrations have combined elements from more than one model to suit the needs or styles of the president, his cabinet, and staff.

Three Policymaking Models

The Centralized Model

- A centralized approach to executive branch decisionmaking generally involves concentrating the policymaking engine in the White House.
  - Under this model, the president's close advisors, supported by a fairly sizable Executive Office staff, are responsible for monitoring, assimilating, and synthesizing information as a basis for forming policy alternatives.
  - Although department and agency input is sought at various levels, the goal is to avoid the potential parochialism and bureaucratic biases of the agencies by relying on White House staff to develop policy proposals rather than soliciting individual agency recommendations.
- The centralized approach encourages consistency and coherence in administration policy. However, it sacrifices the potential value of agency expertise in developing specific policy alternatives. In addition, by apparently devaluing the agencies' capabilities, it may undermine both public confidence in the agencies and agency support for the president.

The Multiple Advocacy Model

- In contrast to the centralized model, a multiple advocacy approach to decisionmaking aims to maximize the potential contributions of the agencies.
  - The key component of this model is an organized, systematized interagency coordination process designed to vet the different views and policy proposals of the agencies.
  - The coordinating mechanism may be based either in the White House or in a particular agency (for economic policy,

Treasury), with either a White House official or a cabinet member serving as principal coordinator.

- The coordinator's task is to draw out the views of the agencies, thereby providing agency leaders with a recognizable stake in the policymaking process, and at the same time to prevent any one agency from exercising undue influence over the recommendations ultimately presented to the president.

- In providing the link between the agencies and the president, the coordinator need not be neutral with respect to the policy alternatives suggested, but should, even while offering his or her own assessment of the options, ensure that the president has the benefit of a balanced and fair representation of the proffered alternatives.

The Ad Hoc Model

- The ad hoc approach to policy coordination eschews formal structures in favor of a flexible, case-by-case mechanism.
  - Under this model, the president may rely, from issue to issue, on his own staff, on the staffs of the individual agencies, or on an ad hoc group for analysis, evaluation, and recommendations.
  - Depending on the scope of an issue, any number of agencies may be tapped to assist in developing policy alternatives.
- A principal advantage of the ad hoc approach is its flexible nature and ability to be "customized" to particular issues.
  - By delegating responsibility for a specific issue-area to those with the most substantive expertise and long-term interest in that issue-area, the ad hoc approach maximizes efficiency and ensures that proposed solutions reflect a solid understanding of the factors at stake.
  - Agency staff who are well grounded in the issue-area may be able to spot problems and, in coordination with other agencies, assess options and propose initial solutions much more readily (and perhaps more reliably) than members of an established White House or cabinet-level group.

- Disadvantages of the ad hoc approach include the risks of dis-
aggregating economic policymaking to such an extent that U.S.
policy lacks consistency and of creating agency resentment and
distrust if individual agencies are not sufficiently drawn into the
decisionmaking process on issues in which they have a stake.

Recent Examples of the Models at Work

The Kennedy Administration

- The Kennedy administration, perhaps more than any other modern administration, relied heavily on ad hoc decisionmaking.
  - President Kennedy strongly favored a flexible policymaking
  apparatus that would be responsive to current needs and not
  limited by structural formalities.
  - In line with this preference, he discontinued both the Advisory Board of Economic Growth and Stability and the Council on Foreign Economic Policy created in the Eisenhower
  administration, which had been responsible, respectively,
  for coordinating domestic and foreign economic policy.
- President Kennedy created several ad hoc committees to deal
with specific domestic economic issues, including a committee
on housing credit, a White House committee on small business,
an advisory committee on labor-management policy, and a fiscal "troika" consisting of the chairman of the CEA, the secretary of the treasury, and the director of the Bureau of the Budget
(BOB).
- International economic policy was generally segregated from
domestic economic policy in the Kennedy administration. To deal
with foreign economic policy issues (other than monetary affairs),
Kennedy generally delegated responsibility to an Interdepart-
mental Committee of Under Secretaries on Foreign Economic
Policy and to his deputy assistant for national security affairs,
Carl Kaysen. Kaysen had a very small White House staff and
worked closely with both the president and the cabinet officers.
  - In 1962, Kennedy also created a cabinet-level Committee
  on Balance of Payments, with a mandate to consider broad
  policy questions and oversee U.S. expenditures abroad.

- Kennedy established the Committee on Balance of Payments without issuing an executive order or other formal constituent document, deliberately avoiding the potential constraints on flexibility such institutionalization might involve.

The Johnson Administration

- President Johnson, while retaining elements of the Kennedy administration's economic policymaking apparatus, including the fiscal troika, established a more centralized economic policymaking process. A single White House staff person—Joseph A. Califano Jr.—was principally responsible from mid-1965 to the end of the administration for both domestic and economic policy.
  - Califano had one assistant on economic policy matters, but relied heavily on the Bureau of the Budget.
  - Johnson did not use the cabinet in any systematic way for policy formulation, although he did tap individual cabinet members (such as the secretaries of Labor and Commerce) on particular policy issues from time to time.
  - Johnson also created ad hoc groups of advisors on fiscal and other macroeconomic issues, but, by generally limiting the members of those groups to the same twelve or fifteen individuals, he effectively centralized even the ad hoc mechanisms he used.

- As was true in the Kennedy administration, the NSC coordinated major international economic policy issues under the direction of Francis M. Bator, who succeeded Carl Kaysen as deputy assistant to the president for national security affairs.

The Nixon Administration

- President Nixon drew on both the multiple advocacy and the centralized decisionmaking models to coordinate economic policy. On the domestic side, he delegated economic responsibilities to, successively, Treasury Secretaries John B. Connally Jr. and George P. Shultz. Virtually all domestic economic proposals, however, were channeled through White House Domestic Advisor John D. Ehrlichman, who exercised a high level of centralized control over final policy decisions.

- Connally worked primarily through the fiscal troika inherited from the Kennedy and Johnson administrations.
- Shultz established interagency committees to handle specific issues.

- On international issues, the NSC under Henry A. Kissinger played much more of a centralized policymaking role than a coordinating role. However, Kissinger and the NSC also did not get extensively involved in international economic issues. President Nixon established a new entity, the Council on International Economic Policy (CIEP), specifically to assume that responsibility.

  - The CIEP, a cabinet-level group chaired first by the president and later by the treasury secretary, was, for all practical purposes, run out of the White House by its executive director (first Peter G. Peterson, then Peter M. Flanigan).
  - The CIEP's relationship to both the Treasury Department and the Special Trade Representative (USTR's predecessor) was somewhat problematic, as Treasury resisted a CIEP role in international monetary decisions and the Special Trade Representative sought to retain control over international trade.

- The CIEP's position was clarified at the beginning of Nixon's second term, when he created the Council on Economic Policy (CEP), which had jurisdiction over domestic and international economics. Nixon designated Treasury Secretary Shultz, whom he also appointed as assistant to the president for economic policy, as the chair of both the CEP and the CIEP. Shultz relied primarily on a small White House staff (headed by Kenneth W. Dam) to execute the work of the CEP.

  - The CEP attempted to facilitate coordination of Treasury's work in international economic policy with that of the CIEP, as well as with the Special Trade Representative's work on international trade matters.
  - The CIEP, however, does not appear to have played a major role in the policymaking process, except on selected trade issues. (Its competition with the Special Trade Representa-

tive and, at times, the NSC ultimately led to its demise: President Carter allowed the CIEP to expire in 1977.)

The Ford Administration

- One of the best examples of a multiple advocacy body formed to coordinate both domestic and international economic policymaking out of the White House is the Ford administration's Economic Policy Board (EPB).[3] The EPB was nominally chaired by the secretary of the treasury, but in practice it served at the direction of its White House–based executive director, L. William Seidman.
    - The EPB's members included the secretaries of Agriculture, Commerce, Health, Education and Welfare, Housing and Urban Development, Interior, Labor, State, Transportation, and Treasury; the director of OMB; the chairman of the CEA; and the executive director of the CIEP.
    - The EPB shared White House advisory responsibilities with the NSC, OMB, the Domestic Council, and the Energy Resources Council. When issues overlapped between these entities, the allocation of responsibilities was generally based on whose function was most closely related to the issue.
    - Because of close communications and good relationships among the individuals who ran these entities, there was generally effective coordination and an efficient division of responsibility among them.
- The EPB engaged in three regular activities. First, it met daily to address issues that needed continuous attention. Second, it convened special meetings to deal with discrete problems (such as New York City finances, the Arab boycott, corporate bribery abroad, and Soviet grain sales). Third, it oversaw long-term projects to address broader issues, such as productivity, capital formation, product liability, and railroad reorganization.
- The EPB's experience has important lessons for the NEC. It demonstrates the strengths of a White House–based multiple advocacy structure, but also signals how important it is for the

3. For an extensive discussion of the EPB, see Porter, *Presidential Decision Making.*

officials who preside over such a structure to balance their control with the contributions of the agencies.

The Carter Administration

- President Carter employed a mix of centralized, multiple advocacy, and ad hoc mechanisms to coordinate economic policy.
    - He created a body similar to, although less formal than, the Nixon CEP: the Economic Policy Group (EPG). The EPG initially was cochaired by Secretary of the Treasury W. Michael Blumenthal and CEA head Charles L. Schultze, though Blumenthal eventually became the sole chair.
    - Like the CEP, the EPG was originally intended to handle both domestic and international economic policy, but in practice it focused almost exclusively on domestic issues because major international economic issues were channeled through the NSC.
    - Over time, the EPG had difficulty controlling even the domestic economic agenda, as President Carter increasingly turned for economic policy advice to the Domestic Policy Staff, led by Domestic Policy Advisor Stuart E. Eizenstat.
- For international economic policymaking, the NSC (principally through Henry Owen) took the lead in coordinating most decisions, especially on U.S. policy at the annual economic summits.

The Reagan Administration

- President Reagan utilized elements of both the centralized and the multiple advocacy models.
- In his first term, Reagan established a range of cabinet councils to coordinate policy, all under the direction of the counsellor to the president, Edwin P. Meese III. The interagency economic coordinating group was the Economic Policy Council (EPC), headed by Treasury Secretary Donald T. Regan.
- The Reagan White House chief of staff, James A. Baker III, formed a Legislative Strategy Group (LSG) that could, in effect, rework policy decisions of the EPC and other cabinet councils as part of the administration's overall legislative strategy.

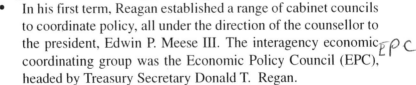

- The LSG included the chief of staff, the counsellor to the president, the deputy chief of staff, the deputy to the chief of staff, and the assistant to the president for legislative affairs, with other officials or agency heads invited as appropriate.
- The LSG was involved heavily in domestic economic issues, but did not focus as much on international economic issues, which were left primarily to the Treasury Department, the EPC, and the NSC.
- In the second Reagan term, with James Baker as treasury secretary, the EPC coordinated domestic and international economic policy under his chairmanship. The Treasury Department itself handled many of the important economic issues for the administration (including those related to international monetary affairs).
  - The EPC was especially active and effective in coordinating U.S. trade policy, including a free trade agreement with Canada, the Uruguay Round multilateral trade negotiations, the 1988 trade legislation, and a range of important trade cases initiated under U.S. law against foreign exporters.
  - The NSC participated in EPC meetings when international matters were discussed.

The Bush Administration

- The Bush administration maintained elements of the multiple advocacy structure established during the Reagan administration but also created its own centralized and ad hoc mechanisms to handle economic policy matters. President Bush retained the EPC but relied on it less substantially than Reagan had, especially for domestic issues.
  - The EPC had a small White House staff, headed by an executive secretary, that generally prepared papers for EPC meetings.
  - However, Bush often turned directly to his OMB director, Richard G. Darman, for economic advice on domestic issues, and also to Chief of Staff John H. Sununu and Treasury Secretary Nicholas F. Brady.

- For international economic policy issues, President Bush utilized the EPC, primarily for trade issues, with strong support from the USTR (under Carla A. Hills) and its interagency coordination of trade issues at the subcabinet level. Bush also looked to the NSC and, when appropriate, the Departments of Treasury and State to coordinate certain international economic initiatives. In several instances, "customized" groups were created to address particular issues.

    - For example, on NAFTA, President Bush combined high-level strategy meetings with his senior foreign policy advisors with coordination by the USTR of interagency groups for policy implementation.
    - When Iraq invaded Kuwait, the administration formed a series of task forces, jointly chaired by Treasury and State, to coordinate issues relating to the use of economic sanctions.
    - The administration also established an interagency mechanism chaired by the State Department to coordinate U.S. assistance to the countries of Central and Eastern Europe and, later, to the countries of the former Soviet Union.
    - These groups were particularly effective because they had a well-defined focus and consisted of individuals with experience and expertise specifically matched to the issues at stake.

3

Assessment and Recommendations

I n assessing the NEC, we have relied primarily on interviews with over sixty government officials from the Clinton administration and prior administrations. Among the topics discussed in our interviews were the process of coordinating economic policy generally; the particular mechanisms used for this purpose by previous administrations and by the Clinton administration (what seemed to work and what did not); the internal operations of the NEC; its relations with other White House entities and with the agencies; the evolution of the NEC during the Clinton administration; the NEC's role in particular economic policy decisions; whether the NEC is an experiment worth retaining; and, if so, whether it should be modified.

We begin our discussion below with preconditions for and benefits of effective coordination. We next address where to locate the economic policy coordinator and how the NEC has performed in integrating economics into foreign and domestic policy. We then consider the role that the NEC can play in assisting the president to establish strategic priorities, the set of prerequisites that we believe are necessary for effective operation of a White House policy coordinating body such as the NEC, and, finally, whether the NEC should be codified by statute. At appropriate points throughout this section of the report, we provide recommendations based on our assessment of the NEC.

Preconditions for Effective Coordination

Precondition 1: Define the Agenda

- Organizational arrangements should be configured to accommodate the substantive issues and decisions that a president and his administration will face and the priorities that he chooses to pursue.
- Creation of an NEC with broad domestic and foreign jurisdiction coincided with increased public anxiety that globalization of the economy and technological change required the U.S. government to give higher priority to promoting the competitive interests of its companies and workers. At the same time, popular pressure to constrain the social role of government shaped the political environment for domestic policymaking.
- As a new administration begins, the trends that underlay the creation of the NEC and defined the environment in which it functioned appear to be continuing. As noted above, on the domestic side, budgetary pressures on social spending have taken more explicit form in the budgets enacted during the three years since 1992. In general, the new administration will have to reconcile all program decisions with the June 1995 commitment to balance the budget in seven years. Specifically, the administration is likely to consider such issues as the following:
  - Revamping the major entitlement programs (medicare, medicaid, and social security) to accommodate demographic trends in the twenty-first century;
  - Implementing welfare reform (possibly determining changes to propose) with a credible approach to preparing welfare recipients for the job market and providing jobs once eligibility has expired;
  - Considering new education and training initiatives to equip workers with the tools to compete for future employment; and
  - Developing incremental health care reform legislation.

- On the international side, the administration will face difficult economic challenges consistent with maintaining U.S. engagement and leadership in the world, including:
  - Sustaining support for the continued liberalization of international trade, including obtaining "fast track" negotiating authority and moving forward on regional free trade arrangements;
  - Attempting to manage the smooth integration into the world economy of China, Russia, and regional powers such as India and Brazil (including in some cases the issue of accession to the World Trade Organization);
  - Addressing the significant financial and political ramifications of European movement toward monetary union (a likely subject for discussion at the 1997 G-7 summit to be held in Denver, Colorado); and
  - Developing internationally effective and domestically sustainable policies on the use of economic sanctions, export controls, and other measures to try to curb terrorism and the proliferation of weapons of mass destruction.

RECOMMENDATION: The new administration should retain the NEC or establish a body with a similar mission. The agenda of issues facing the president in the next term provides an ample basis for having a mechanism to integrate economic considerations into coherent domestic and foreign policies.

Precondition 2: Pick a Team, Not Simply Players

- A significant contributing factor to the collegial environment among NEC members came before President Clinton even was inaugurated. During the transition, President Clinton selected the key NEC members and the NEC advisor as an "economic team."
  - Several members of the team had previously worked together and with the president.
  - Each brought to the table valuable but differing expertise; some were financiers, some were economists, some were active in the election campaign, and two had chaired congressional committees deeply involved in economic policy.

- The general views that each held about economic policy priorities were broadly compatible with those of other members of the team and with those of the president.
- Other administrations with records of particularly smooth top-level coordination reflect a similar pattern.
  - A good example was President Bush's national security team, which included Brent Scowcroft (an NSC advisor with stature, a close relationship to the president, and a penchant for keeping a low profile); Secretary of State James A. Baker III; Secretary of Defense Richard Cheney; and Chairman of the Joint Chiefs of Staff Colin L. Powell. Having served with each other in different positions in previous administrations, these individuals possessed, in addition to their individual expertise, a high degree of mutual respect, friendship, and admiration that enhanced their ability to work together, even when they did not always agree on issues. President Clinton expressly sought to model the composition and operation of his economic team after the Bush NSC team.
  - As George Shultz and Kenneth Dam have written: "No substitute for individual ability can be found in organizational diagrams. Team spirit may be regarded by academics and pundits as a hackneyed concept, but nothing is more important for effective policymaking, especially in difficult periods."[4]
- Presidents who have overlooked this point when filling key positions often have been obliged to deal with chronic tensions and conflict.
  - President Carter, for example, named to his cabinet and key subcabinet posts a number of individuals with an equivocal commitment to the administration as a whole, policy agendas that differed from his, and resistance to sharing power or taking into account other views or interests.
  - The result was frequent, sometimes public fractiousness and internal opposition to presidential policies that hampered the performance of the administration.

4. Shultz and Dam, *Economic Policy beyond the Headlines, p.* 159.

RECOMMENDATION: To enable the NEC and other economic entities to coordinate policy effectively, the president should place the highest priority on forming a team with complementary skills, mutually accepted roles, and the expertise necessary to address his agenda. It also is critical to select as NEC advisor (and NSC advisor and DPC advisor) individuals who combine "gravitas" with a "no-sharp-elbows" management style.

Benefits of Effective Coordination

Benefit 1: Vetting Proposals

- The single greatest return that a president receives from investing in an effective coordination process is the assurance that thorough "debugging" occurs before he embraces proposals, embodies them in regulations, submits them to Congress, or takes other action.
- The evidence from the Clinton administration is graphic. A number of administration officials felt that initiatives subjected to the coordination process generally fared well and those that were not vetted often failed.
- The most prominent example of productive NEC coordination is the first: the development of the five-year deficit reduction package, including a proposed budget for fiscal year 1994 containing numerous new programs and revisions of existing programs, as well as a $16 billion economic stimulus package, submitted to Congress on February 17, 1993.
  - This NEC-led process required the president and his key advisors to prioritize the proposals championed during his campaign and subject them to the discipline of the budget process—all within a compressed time frame.
  - In this process, the administration made a fundamental decision: to make long-term deficit reduction and low interest rates a central strategic priority.
    - This decision entailed deferring the middle-class tax cuts that were a significant campaign priority.
    - Favoring deficit reduction also meant subordinating the important campaign goal of increasing public invest-

ment in infrastructure and human capital; the Clinton budget submitted to Congress provided significantly less funding for new public investment programs than the president had originally anticipated, and Congress cut his public investment proposals much further, almost to zero.

- Although this choice of priorities was difficult for key members of the administration (and important constituencies), the process provided all players with the opportunity to identify the options, grasp their consequences, press individual views, and ultimately accept and support the president's decisions.

- In view of the fact that the budget plan encountered serious unanticipated difficulties after reaching Capitol Hill, including rejection of the economic stimulus package, before the overall plan passed by razor-thin margins, it appears that the NEC process may not have given adequate attention to the politics of the issues considered. But overall, especially given the fact that the plan was (of necessity) submitted to Congress less than a month after NEC members moved into their offices, the process of developing this budget plan served the president well.

- In addition to the 1993 budget exercise, other examples of effective coordination include:

  - The 1993 decision to press for enactment of legislation implementing the NAFTA: following the negotiation of labor and environmental side agreements for the NAFTA, the NEC managed a process that focused the administration's attention on passing the implementing legislation. The importance of the NEC's role was enhanced because passage of the NAFTA legislation was a particularly high-stakes exercise: as one senior Clinton official observed, had the president challenged congressional Democrats and lost, his leadership would have been significantly undermined.

  - The conclusion of the Uruguay Round Multilateral Trade Negotiations and its implementing legislation: again, the NEC played an important role in focusing administration attention on this key trade initiative.

  - The president's June 1995 seven-year balanced budget package: for one month after the president decided to make such a proposal, the NEC undertook an intensive and confidential interagency process of reviewing options. The result was that, after the president unveiled his complex proposal, no major mistakes or embarrassing complications turned up. Moreover, during the period of review by the NEC, there were no leaks to the press that the president already had decided to propose his own seven-year balanced budget plan, thus evidencing the loyalty of participants to this NEC-managed process.

- The proposals announced in the president's "Middle Class Bill of Rights" speech in December 1994: the NEC coordinated consideration of tax incentives targeted at education, child care, home ownership, and health needs, and a voucher program for worker retraining.

- Several of the policy initiatives announced by the president during the second and third quarters of 1996: the chief of staff asked the NEC to vet and refine concepts, including some proposed by consultant Dick Morris, for additional tax incentives and new environmental and education-related proposals. (Numerous other ideas also were vetted, but were found to be unworkable and were discarded.) One official stressed that the NEC was able to coordinate these proposals rapidly because by 1996 NEC members were accustomed to working cooperatively and efficiently with each other.

- The Clinton administration also provides graphic illustrations of major policy initiatives that were not subjected to broad interagency scrutiny and that, partly as a result, failed.

  - The initial China MFN policy: in June 1993, the president, acting on the advice of the NSC and the State Department, but without significant involvement by the NEC, announced his policy of conditioning most-favored-nation (MFN) status for China on an annual review of China's progress in improving its human rights record. This policy proved to be untenable. China found the threat of revoking MFN treatment noncredible, and the president ultimately decided that following through on the threat would be disproportionately damaging to U.S. economic interests. After a year of what appeared to the public as vacillation in U.S. policy, the NEC and the NSC jointly recommended, and the president endorsed, eliminating the link for China between MFN and progress in the area of human rights.

- The 1994 health care reform proposal: according to many administration officials, one of the most basic problems encountered by the health care reform proposal was an absence of serious or systematic internal consultation along the lines of the NEC process. One official equated some aspects of the process of designing the Clinton health plan to the process by which the Carter administration drafted its ill-fated first energy plan immediately following president Carter's inauguration—"developing a major policy initiative in a broom closet."

- Officials who served in prior administrations have similarly testified to the value of effective vetting and the potentially disastrous costs of short-circuiting the coordinating process.

  - A particularly telling example is provided by an experience of the Ford administration and its Economic Policy Board (EPB). In one instance, President Ford decided that EPB coordination was not necessary, as Labor Secretary John T. Dunlop assured him that he could resolve a highly contentious labor-management issue with a legislative proposal that both business and organized labor would accept. Having some knowledge of the issue himself, and in view of the apparent fact that both parties to the controversy would have to sign on to the proposal before the administration would accept it, President Ford authorized Dunlop to proceed on his own. Ford ultimately embraced the resulting labor-management compromise and submitted it to Congress.

  - At that point, representatives of the Associated General Contractors of America, who had not been parties to the deal brokered by Dunlop, voiced angry opposition. Treasury Secretary William E. Simon threatened to resign if the administration did not withdraw its support for the proposal. The president was obliged to do just that. As a result, Labor Secretary Dunlop resigned, and the AFL-CIO, greatly angered, significantly intensified its opposition to President Ford's reelection.

Benefit 2: Exposing the President to All Sides of Controversies

- A second benefit of effective coordination is that it provides the president with the opportunity to hear, directly, the case for different sides of critical policy debates. President Ford frequently attended meetings of his EPB and, according to one participant, relied heavily on "disciplined debate" among its members for getting the information he needed to make decisions.
- NEC members interviewed for this report noted that President Clinton has frequently attended NEC meetings to listen to and participate in policy debates. Several cited an August 1993 meeting in which the president heard a vigorous discussion about assigning top priority to enactment of the NAFTA implementing legislation. After what was described as a particularly compelling pro-NAFTA speech by Treasury Secretary Bentsen, President Clinton announced his decision to wage an intensive campaign for the implementing legislation.

Benefit 3: Minimizing Turf Competition

- A third benefit of coordination is preventing individual agencies from "hoarding" the policy agenda. All veterans of government know the resilience of the tendency of individual departments and agencies to focus on preserving or expanding their jurisdiction, promoting their traditional pet policy ideas and programs, and addressing the interests of their particular constituencies.
- In general, the longer that political appointees, from cabinet members on down, serve in their positions, the more they tend to be prone to "capture" by the agencies they head, and to embrace comparatively parochial agendas, sometimes at the expense of the president's agenda.
- A working, frequently used coordinating process, such as the NEC, the Ford EPB, or the Bush NSC, is one of the most effective antidotes to this common tendency toward calcification of agency positions.

Benefit 4: Closing Ranks behind Presidential Decisions

- When a president makes a controversial decision, the last thing he needs is for the losers of the internal debate to undercut his policy through leaking and covert advocacy. The Clinton NEC process generally appears to have been effective in minimizing this common threat to presidential leadership. One official summed up the widespread view that "members felt they had their shot at influencing the president on his decisions and thus were willing to accept those decisions that went against them."

- Similar sentiments were expressed by members of President Bush's national security team and by participants in President Ford's EPB process.

Benefit 5: Harnessing the Information and Analytical Resources of the Government

- New administrations in both parties have a tendency to reinvent the wheel, tackling major issues anew without taking advantage of the experience and expertise potentially at their disposal in the federal government. Effective interagency coordination should enable a president and his close advisors to draw on the networks of information and analytical power in the Executive Office and the federal departments and agencies.
- Many officials with whom we spoke observed that the NEC sometimes performed this function well, directly plugging economic policy experts at CEA, OMB, Treasury, Labor, and other agencies into presidential decisionmaking.
- A number of officials, however, felt that the NEC's record on utilizing available analytical resources within the agencies was mixed and was generally thin with regard to strategic planning. One official observed: "There was a lot of ad hoc-ery and a lot of firepower kicking around the administration that was not consistently used in the service of strategic planning."

Benefit 6: Providing Outreach and Gathering Intelligence

- Effective interagency coordination provides the president not only with the views of the agencies but also, implicitly and explicitly, with the sentiments, expectations, and priorities of the constituencies associated with individual agencies and programs.
- White House policy advisors also can make a critical contribution to an administration's effectiveness by engaging in outreach and gathering intelligence. Business, labor, environmental, and other interest group leaders often "connect" most effectively with top policy officials.

- The top White House economic policy coordinator in a Republican administration told us that he spent at least half of his day meeting with business and labor leaders, and, specifically, that he met with leaders of the AFL-CIO in their offices on a biweekly basis.
- In part because of his previous ties to Wall Street, NEC Advisor Robert Rubin was effective at staying in touch with the financial community and thus being able to anticipate how Clinton administration initiatives might affect the financial markets.

Locating the Economic Policy Coordinator

- In the area of national security, the interagency coordinator in modern administrations has consistently been located at the White House in the person of the NSC advisor.[5] In contrast, with respect to economic policy, presidents have configured their mechanisms for interagency coordination in a number of different ways.
- Although several previous administrations have made the treasury secretary the formal head of economic policy coordinating entities, these cases do not necessarily offer persuasive support for the proposition that interagency coordination can, in fact, be managed effectively from Treasury.
    - In several instances, treasury secretaries have used the interagency coordinating process sparingly, preferring instead—sometimes with excellent results—to manage economic policy primarily from the Treasury Department. In the case of the Ford EPB, where Treasury Secretary William Simon "chaired" an extremely active and operational interagency coordinating mechanism, Simon's role as chair seems, in fact, to have been mainly ceremonial.
        - William Seidman directed the operations of the EPB from his West Wing office, setting the agendas for the

5. The quasi-exception proves the rule: When Henry Kissinger, the NSC advisor at the outset of the Nixon administration, became secretary of state, he kept his NSC position. This situation, however, eventually proved to be unworkable, and President Ford named Kissinger's deputy, Brent Scowcroft, to be the NSC advisor, with Kissinger remaining the secretary of state.

daily meetings of the EPB Executive Committee, running the meetings, managing the interagency task forces created to staff issues, and serving as presidential liaison to significant economic constituencies from the business and organized labor communities.

- Seidman kept an even lower public profile than Robert Rubin did as NEC advisor, but in fact he appears to have played an equally significant role.

- In the Nixon administration, Treasury Secretary George Shultz was an active coordinator of the Council on Economic Policy. But President Nixon had given Shultz a second position, that of assistant to the president for economic affairs. It was in this second role that Shultz coordinated the administration's economic policy. Shultz started each day in his White House office, and he conducted all interagency meetings in the White House, in order to avoid raising anxieties of other cabinet members about his capacity to be an honest broker.

- In the Clinton administration, the informal structure of economic policy coordination changed after Leon Panetta became White House chief of staff.

  - Having previously served as OMB director and, before that, as chair of the House Budget Committee, Panetta had unique expertise in the budgetary process at the very time that the federal budget became the overriding issue facing the White House.

  - Panetta and the Budget Strategy Group that he chaired became the "nerve center" of budget policy and strategy development, while the NEC continued to coordinate other issues, especially in the international economic policy area.

  - NEC Advisor Laura Tyson also assumed an unusually visible public role as an administration spokesperson on economic policy matters, in part because of her skill in this area and in part because the treasury secretary was comfortable having her do this. Tyson's experience contravenes the conventional wisdom that a White House economic advisor should maintain a low public profile while the treasury secretary should be the administration's chief economic spokesman.

- The foregoing should serve as a caution to anyone inclined to proclaim as an ironclad rule that the presidential policy coordinating function "must" be run from a particular bureaucratic location, or that economic policy responsibilities must be allocated in a particular manner among the major players (treasury secretary, OMB director, White House economic advisor, White House domestic advisor, NSC advisor, CEA chair). Although we reject any such limitation on structural options, we believe certain conclusions are justified by the experience of the Clinton administration and its predecessors.
- Interagency coordination should, with perhaps rare exceptions, be managed by an official in the Executive Office of the President. Cabinet officers such as the treasury secretary, if given this responsibility, often are perceived as promoting their own agendas relative to those of other agencies. Cabinet officers also may have difficulty linking the coordination process directly to the policy and political priorities of the president.
- Within the Executive Office, the White House is generally a more advantageous place than OMB to locate a strong presidential interagency coordinator.
  - Although OMB views its mission as requiring fairness and objectivity, and although OMB has substantial, sophisticated, and broad-gauged analytical capacity, many agency officials tend to view OMB less as a neutral honest broker than as a player preoccupied with trimming the federal budget. Several agency representatives told us that in meetings chaired by OMB officials they tend to feel more constrained than in meetings chaired by White House officials.
  - A high priority for every agency involves its annual negotiation with OMB over its own budget; some of those interviewed observed that, if OMB is the interagency policy coordinator, either the agencies or OMB might be tempted to find ways to use the coordinating process to gain leverage in their budget negotiations.
  - A White House–based coordinator is usually in a better position than the OMB director to play the role of "keeper of the flame," ensuring a close fit between administration actions and the president's policy and political agenda.

- Managing the budget process and other functions of OMB is a large responsibility in itself that probably would detract from the priority attention that the OMB director could give to coordination of nonbudget issues.
- In the relatively unusual cases where OMB directors have served as the president's chief economic policy coordinator, the OMB director in question had an extensive economic policy and political background, and the administration's main economic and domestic policy priorities were fundamentally entwined with the budget.

- Although a White House chief of staff with the appropriate expertise can manage interagency policy development, directly or indirectly through a strong deputy, it generally will be advantageous to assign the process management function to a senior presidential assistant other than the chief of staff.
  - The chief of staff's crisis-management responsibilities and the span of his mandate are likely to undermine his ability to keep a coordinating process operating consistently and successfully.
  - The value of assigning the coordinating function to a discrete Executive Office entity (such as the NEC), rather than the chief of staff, becomes even greater as the complexity of a given president's economic policy agenda increases.

RECOMMENDATION: The NEC should continue to be directed by an assistant to the president for economic affairs who is located in the West Wing of the White House. A discrete White House entity such as the NEC is the preferred base from which to coordinate economic policy.

Making Economics Count in Foreign Policy

Background

- Although geopolitical and security considerations often overshadow U.S. economic interests in the formulation of U.S. foreign policy, that is not always the case.
  - The Marshall Plan to reconstruct post–World War II Europe, the formation of the International Monetary Fund and

the World Bank, the creation of the General Agreement on Tariffs and Trade, the successive rounds of multilateral trade negotiations, the multifaceted response to the oil crisis of the early 1970s, and the policy initiatives designed to deal with the third world debt crises of the 1980s are but a few examples of significant and successful international economic policymaking.

- In many of these instances, the making of such policy has been widely viewed as tantamount to the pursuit of national security objectives, and the decisionmaking apparatus within the executive branch has thus readily integrated these economic factors in shaping foreign policy.

- However, most (but not all) of those interviewed felt that, during the past four decades, integration of economic considerations into the development and execution of U.S. foreign policy has been sporadic and uneven.

- There is a widespread perception that a significant cause of the comparative lack of priority given to international economic issues has been that foreign economic policy has been a bureaucratic orphan.

  - The national security bureaucracies and the officials who inhabit them, including the NSC, have as their overriding concerns political and military affairs.

  - Domestic policy agencies, White House domestic policy coordinators, and OMB view economics as a priority, but (other than the Department of the Treasury) they have had comparatively less focus on or expertise in economic matters outside U.S. national borders.

- In recent years, however, the progressive reductions of barriers to trade and the accelerated globalization of the international economy have begun to solidify consensus on a definition of "foreign relations" that reflects the consolidation and integration of geopolitical, security, *and* economic considerations.

  - The presidential directive establishing the NEC acknowledged the need "to coordinate the economic policy-making process with respect to domestic and international economic issues." In other words, underlying the creation of the NEC was the dual premise that U.S. national security is, in part, a function of economic policy, and that U.S. domestic economic strength is, in part, a function of foreign policy.

- Thus, the assistant to the president for economic policy is directed to work in conjunction with the assistant to the president for national security.
- In the Clinton administration, the core group of NEC deputies coordinating foreign economic policy has included representatives from the Departments of State, Treasury, and Commerce; from the USTR; and, more recently, from the Departments of Agriculture and Labor. During the first two years of the Clinton administration, the NEC deputies focused heavily on trade policy; more recently, they have devoted increased time to other international economic issues as well.

The NEC's Principal Focus: International Trade Policy

- As has been the case with many previous economic coordinating bodies, the NEC has participated more consistently and aggressively in international trade policy than any other single policy area.
  - This is not surprising, because trade policy increasingly affects a broad range of domestic interests and received considerable emphasis during the 1992 Clinton campaign.
  - Moreover, the Clinton administration confronted at its outset major trade policy issues, such as the enactment of legislation implementing the NAFTA, the conclusion of the Uruguay Round negotiations, and the establishment of a framework for trade negotiations with Japan.
- In formulating trade policy, previous administrations have made extensive use of the interagency coordinating mechanisms chaired by the USTR—the Trade Policy Staff Committee (TPSC) and the Trade Policy Review Group (TPRG)—before elevating major decisions to the cabinet level.[6]

---

6. Since 1975, the interagency coordination of trade policy has been designed to occur at three levels: the office director level, through the TPSC (which has many subgroups on specific issues); the under secretary and assistant secretary levels, through the TPRG; and the cabinet secretary level, through the Trade Policy Committee (TPC). Congress has designated the USTR as having the primary responsibility for coordinating the development and implementation of trade policy with other agencies. In practice, most administrations have used some mechanism other than the TPC to coordinate cabinet-level decisions on trade policy.

- The TPSC undertakes initial staff work on trade issues and has a number of subcommittees organized around particular subjects. The more important trade issues—often those that are the subject of disagreement—are then considered by the TPRG. Both groups are chaired by a representative from the USTR and usually consist of representatives from the Departments of State, Treasury, Commerce, Defense, Labor, Agriculture, Interior, Transportation, Energy, and Justice, with participation as well from OMB, CEA, the NSC, and the Agency for International Development. The USTR attempts to forge compromises among these various bodies, but has the authority, underscored by statute, to make independent recommendations to the president.
- In the Reagan and Bush administrations, the USTR often chaired interagency subcabinet deliberations and on many occasions was able to resolve trade policy issues at the TPRG level. The USTR would elevate major issues within its jurisdiction (such as trade agreements and high-profile trade cases under U.S. law) to the cabinet level (generally the EPC) and thereby emphasize the important strategic or foreign policy implications of these issues.
- Indeed, the Reagan and Bush administrations were quite active in successfully launching several such major trade initiatives on a bilateral basis (U.S.-Israel Free Trade Agreement, U.S.-Canada Free Trade Agreement), a regional basis (NAFTA, APEC, the Enterprise for the Americas), and a multilateral basis (Uruguay Round trade negotiations).
- The process for formulating trade policy has changed considerably during the Clinton administration.
  - Meetings of the NEC deputies have effectively supplanted—or, in the words of one (non-USTR) official, "undercut"—the TPRG as the primary forum for resolving trade issues.
  - The USTR's role has shifted from serving as chair of the interagency process to serving as policy advocate within the NEC and as the operational implementer of negotiating goals and strategies developed by the NEC.
- The NEC appears to have reproduced some of the same salutary effects of trade policy coordination as in previous administrations. First, like the Reagan and Bush administrations, the NEC

has given priority and visibility to trade policy, consistently making that policy a matter of cabinet-level concern. Members of the Clinton administration have praised this NEC function.

- One senior official, for example, suggested that other cabinet members would not have been as eager to attend coordinating meetings had they been chaired by Mickey Kantor at USTR's headquarters rather than by the NEC in the Roosevelt Room of the White House.
- Several officials have stated that the intense involvement of NEC principals in the NAFTA issue contributed significantly to the president's August 1993 decision to move NAFTA approval ahead of health care as the administration's top priority for the fall of that year.
- Officials in the Clinton administration also cited the NEC's critical role in bringing together the interests of concerned agencies to develop a comprehensive framework for approaching U.S.-Japanese trade negotiations. The NEC process led, in some (but not all) instances, to a more balanced and less aggressive posture toward Japanese trade issues than might have been the case had the USTR acted on its own.
- Another benefit of using the NEC to coordinate trade policy— similar to the benefit of cabinet-level backing in the Reagan and Bush administrations—was to enhance the posture of U.S. trade negotiators. With top-level, administration-wide backing, U.S. negotiators felt great confidence in the positions they took to the table in Geneva and Tokyo.
- However, although the NEC has provided an effective forum for the deputies and principals on these issues, several officials with whom we spoke expressed concern about the diminished role of the TPRG and criticized the NEC for becoming involved too early and too often in the policymaking process. We understand that NEC officials have begun in recent months to take steps to delegate back to the TPRG more responsibility for interagency coordination of trade issues at early stages in policy development.

RECOMMENDATION: The NEC should continue to revitalize the role of the Trade Policy Review Group in resolving issues that

do not merit attention of the NEC deputies and to provide improved preparatory work for those issues considered by the deputies and principals.

The NEC's Record on International Issues Other Than Trade

- Outside the trade area, the NEC appears to have made its presence felt on a comparatively ad hoc and less consistent basis. The primary (nontrade) international economic issues on which the NEC has played a role, either as a coordinator or as a participant, include:

  - *Export controls.* This is an area in which the Department of Defense has traditionally differed from (and often prevailed over) the Commerce Department in insisting on a broad range of export controls and in giving relatively low weight to U.S. commercial interests in export decisions. In assuming coordinating responsibility for this issue, the NEC has shifted the balance more toward promoting U.S. commercial interests, exemplified by a series of administration decisions significantly decontrolling exports of computers and supercomputers and streamlining export licensing procedures.

  - *Economic sanctions.* Significant sanctions issues arose between 1993 and 1996 in the context of the China MFN debate and in the form of the Helms-Burton legislation relating to Cuba and sanctions legislation relating to Libya and Iran. The latter two legislative measures, which mandate secondary boycotts and directly affect activities of foreign companies, have been widely criticized by U.S. allies as violating basic norms of international trade. Although many members of the NEC opposed such sanctions, we heard that the NEC, at least initially, encountered resistance to its participation in sanctions deliberations and "had to force its way to the table." Perhaps due in part to criticism of the use of unilateral sanctions, the NEC and NSC deputies have now established a process by which all sanctions issues will be coordinated.

  - *Foreign bribery and corruption.* The NEC has coordinated

policy analyses of the impact on U.S. competitiveness of bribery and corruption abroad. These analyses have contributed to U.S. efforts to develop multilateral guidelines forbidding corrupt payments to foreign government officials.

- The NEC has generally avoided (as have economic bodies in previous administrations) seeking to coordinate issues that are largely under one department's control, such as Treasury's handling of international monetary affairs (including exchange rate issues), which are market-sensitive, require technical expertise, and probably are best left out of the interagency process.

- Given the fact that the NEC has been establishing its credibility during the past four years, it was prudent—and, in some cases, entirely appropriate—for it to avoid issues primarily within the competence of a single agency. However, a number of international issues presumptively within the exclusive domain of a particular cabinet secretary may well be ripe for interagency review and coordination.

  - For example, despite Treasury's traditional reluctance to put issues into an interagency coordinating process, some matters within Treasury's jurisdiction—such as the handling of third world debt or the development policies of international financial institutions—have broad foreign policy implications that might well be appropriate for interagency consideration.

  - Another important issue, now handled primarily by the State Department, that might benefit from a measure of interagency consideration is foreign assistance. There are broad economic, political, and national security implications of overall assistance programs to countries in the Middle East, Central and Eastern Europe, and the region of the former Soviet Union.

RECOMMENDATION: The NEC staff should devote additional attention to monitoring agency review of international economic issues, at times stimulating such review on an interagency basis or requesting selected issue-specific materials from the agencies, in an effort to spot emerging issues (or those defined by vigorous debate) that may merit NEC involvement.

The G-7 Summits

- One of the major efforts at international economic coordination is the annual meeting of the leaders of the major industrialized nations, the G-7 summit. Traditionally, one senior U.S. government official—known as the "sherpa"—has had responsibility for overseeing this process.
  - In some administrations, the G-7 sherpa has been based at the NSC; in others, at the State Department.
  - In the Clinton administration, the responsibilities of the G-7 sherpa initially were given to a member of the joint NEC/NSC international economics staff (senior director Robert C. Fauver), were later transferred to Assistant Secretary of State Daniel K. Tarullo in his capacity as a personal representative of the president, and, when Tarullo became NEC deputy, were retained by him.
  - Although the G-7 sherpa process has generally worked well during the Clinton administration, we found no consensus on where the G-7 sherpa should be based: in State, at the NSC, at the NEC, or possibly even at the Treasury Department. (Similarly, there were widely divergent views on the ongoing merits of the annual G-7 summit in its current format.)
  - There was strong consensus, however, that the G-7 sherpa should be sufficiently senior in stature to be able to mobilize interagency coordination and sufficiently close to the president to be viewed as his personal representative. We agree with that perspective.

Alternatives for Integrating Economics with Foreign Policy

- The issue of how best to integrate economic considerations into foreign policy decisions has been given attention by most modern administrations but without a fully satisfactory resolution.
  - Under both Presidents Kennedy and Johnson, there was an effort to coordinate international economics through the National Security Council, by appointing an NSC deputy to specialize in economic issues: first, Carl Kaysen and later, Francis Bator. Henry Owen played a similar role within the

Carter administration's NSC. While many have praised these individuals as effectively coordinating foreign economic policy, some have considered their impact on policy to be uneven. Other presidents and NSC advisors abandoned the practice of designating an NSC deputy to concentrate on international economics.

- The Nixon administration initially had no process dedicated specifically to the coordination of international economic policy. In 1971, the Council on International Economic Policy (CIEP) was created to fill this void. The CIEP was run by an executive director and had a sizable White House staff of more than twenty professionals. But the CIEP, even though codified in statute in 1972, never developed significant influence with either President Nixon or President Ford, and its statutory authorization was allowed to expire at the beginning of the Carter administration.

- The Reagan administration relied on an interagency Economic Policy Council (EPC), led by the Treasury Department, to coordinate domestic and international economic issues. Although the EPC was active at different points in the administration, especially on trade policy, the Treasury Department also played a strong role in many of the important economic issues during Reagan's second term.

- In the Bush administration, agencies such as Treasury, State, Commerce, and the USTR took the lead in their respective international economic areas, with the EPC, the NSC, or other "customized groups" providing coordination as necessary at the senior level.

- Most (but not all) of those with whom we spoke felt that none of these mechanisms had consistently integrated international economics into foreign policy.

- Several of those interviewed were of the view that strengthening the economics capacity of the NSC was a better approach to integrating economics into foreign policy than creating a new coordinating entity such as the NEC.

  - Proponents of this view believe that promoting economic concerns from within the national security community has, when attempted, proved more effective than is commonly perceived.

- They also contend that, given the NSC's predominant role in foreign policy decisionmaking and its large institutional presence, trying to force economics into the mix of foreign policy considerations from outside the NSC will never work.
- Also noted was concern about increased bureaucratic friction and balkanization within the White House.

• However, a substantial majority of those we interviewed—representing both Democratic and Republican administrations—believe that the NSC (and the State Department) are inherently likely to give low priority to economic considerations and that the record casts doubt on the notion that purely internal NSC reform can entirely solve this problem.

• We conclude that the record of the NEC—especially in the area of trade policy, but also on other international issues in which it has become involved—demonstrates that a separate White House–based economic coordinating entity, operating at the top levels with strong presidential support, can make economics count more in foreign policymaking and can enhance communication and coordination between the national security agencies and the economic agencies.

- As one senior NSC official stated, the NSC may, at any point in time, become preoccupied with the security aspects of an uprising in the Middle East, an international terrorist incident, or a military decision on the use of force. Under those circumstances, it is "reassuring to know that an assistant to the president [the NEC advisor] is coordinating agencies to consider the economic ramifications related to those foreign decisions," as well as continuing to provide senior White House attention to other international economic issues.
- State Department officials with economic responsibilities emphasized that the existence of the NEC strengthened their leverage within the department to promote economic issues.
- Senior officials in NEC member agencies unanimously stated that they believe the collective ability of the economic side of the government to influence foreign policymaking is enhanced significantly by the existence of the NEC. "The NEC invites Commerce and Treasury to a meeting where the NSC might not do so."

- The presence of a senior presidential advisor with an economic policy portfolio, who has the confidence of the president and a mandate to advise on international matters, serves to assure that the president and other White House decisionmakers will hear the economic perspective on foreign policy issues, if necessary in competition with the views of the national security establishment.

RECOMMENDATION: Given the widespread bipartisan consensus that the current international environment requires a heightened emphasis on the economic dimensions of foreign policy, the new administration should take the steps noted elsewhere in this report to: (i) retain the NEC and strengthen its coordinating process, (ii) strengthen the economics capacity of the NSC, and (iii) reduce unnecessary friction between the two entities.

Cooperation between the NEC and the NSC

- If the NEC is to continue to be involved in international economics—as we think it should—then steps must be taken to improve coordination between the NEC and the NSC.
- From the inception of the NEC, senior officials of the NEC and of the NSC have understood that cooperation between the two entities would be both crucial to the success of international economic policymaking and difficult to achieve in practice. Several factors reflect this understanding:
    - During the transition, top officials at the NSC and the NEC agreed to use a joint "dual-hatted" staff on international economic issues in order to minimize turf-driven tendencies to generate competing approaches and proposals to common issues.
    - NSC Deputy Sandy Berger, unlike the typical NSC advisor or deputy, has a strong background in international trade and thus is familiar with the nature and significance of international commercial and economic matters.
    - Berger and NEC Deputy Bo Cutter had worked together in the Carter administration. Berger and Cutter, and later Cutter's successor, Dan Tarullo, have maintained frequent

contact throughout the course of the administration. These sorts of informal personal relationships are quite important in reinforcing formal structural relationships.

- On major issues involving significant attention from senior officials and the president, the NEC and the NSC appear frequently to have worked well together. One example is U.S. policy toward Japan.

  - Early in the Clinton administration, the NEC and the NSC jointly chaired a series of deputies' meetings addressing America's relationship with Japan. Within both bodies, a consensus emerged, supported by the president, that the United States needed to get tougher with Japan regarding the trade imbalance between the two countries. This consensus laid the foundation for the framework developed for market-opening negotiations with the Japanese.

  - Later in the Clinton administration, the NEC and the NSC, again acting jointly, decided (in part jolted by events in Okinawa) to shift this initial focus on economic relations with Japan—which they felt had been successful—toward greater emphasis on the security relationship. Accordingly, President Clinton stressed the importance of the U.S.-Japan defense relationship during his trip to Tokyo in early 1996.

  - Of course, good coordination does not guarantee that everyone will view the outcome as good policy, and there are strong critics of the Clinton administration's overall approach to Japan. Such criticism, however, should not be attributed to an internal failure by the Clinton administration to consult and coordinate, but rather reflects substantive disagreements between the critics and the administration.

- There are other times, however, when criticism of the Clinton foreign policy does, at least in part, reflect a lack of effective coordination between the NEC and the NSC. A case in point is policy toward China.

  - Several officials concurred that the Clinton administration's 1993 decision on MFN for China—to link the annual renewal of MFN status to "overall, significant progress" by China on human rights and in other areas—was made between the NSC and the State Department, without significant involvement by the NEC or its constituent economic agencies. After this decision, members of the NEC expressed concern that conditioning renewal of MFN on progress on human rights was an ineffective strategy that could cause disproportionate damage to the U.S. economy.

- Indeed, open discord appeared within the administration on China policy, epitomized by an incident in March 1994 when a senior Commerce Department official was in China promoting U.S. business at the same time that a senior State Department official was there condemning human rights violations.

- When the MFN issue was up for annual renewal in the summer of 1994, the NEC participated fully with the NSC in reassessing U.S. policy. Together, these bodies recommended that the initial policy of conditional renewal of MFN status be abandoned in favor of annual renewal without the imposition of extra conditions beyond the scope of current law, a course that President Clinton endorsed.

- Eventually, the NSC and the NEC jointly attempted to pull administration policies and activities regarding China together by initiating a series of meetings among principals. Although a number of foreign policy experts remain critical of U.S. policy toward China, these meetings seem to have provided a degree of greater coherence to that policy.

- In short, although the NSC has generally sought to collaborate and coordinate with the NEC in advising the president on U.S. foreign policy, this process has not always worked smoothly.

- Collaboration and cooperation between the NEC and the NSC appear to have been particularly difficult to achieve, on a consistent basis, with regard to day-to-day matters over which the NSC has by tradition exercised control but nevertheless involve economic issues.

- Examples are presidential meetings with foreign heads of state or other officials, NSC memoranda to the president on various issues, and NSC briefing materials for the president. Although the NEC usually is ultimately able to provide input on these matters, in the words of one NEC member, "we often have some difficulty pushing our way into the system."

RECOMMENDATION:

- *Because the NEC is better situated than the NSC to reach out to all economic agencies, it should continue to coordinate international economic issues. At the same time, the NSC needs to become more receptive to the economic perspective.*

- *The use by the NEC and the NSC of a dual-hatted staff for international economics has been widely regarded as successful. This practice has increased coordination between the two entities and precluded the development of separate international economic policies by two different staffs. We recommend that this practice continue.*

- *We considered the possibility of creating a dual-hatted deputy, but most of those with whom we spoke rejected that notion, believing that it would be too burdensome for one person to hold such a demanding position and that it would eliminate the potential benefit of providing competing voices at a senior level to present significantly different perspectives on a foreign policy issue. We agree with this perspective, but also recommend that either the NSC advisor or the NSC deputy be familiar with, and sensitive to, international economic matters, as has been the case with the current NSC deputy.*

- *Among other steps that the NSC could take to increase its receptivity to coordination with the NEC, we recommend the following:*

    - *The NSC secretariat should work closely with a newly created, three-person NEC secretariat to ensure a full sharing of briefing papers and other background material, the provision of NEC clearances on all papers drafted by the NSC having economic components or implications, the drafting of written instructions based on joint NEC/NSC meetings, and the circulation of those instructions to appropriate agencies for implementation.*

    - *The NSC advisor should seek to have on the staff of the regional directorates (where most of policy is actually coordinated) some individuals who have expertise in economic, commercial, or financial affairs.*

    - *We realize that providing additional economics capabilities within the NSC in order to strengthen coordination with the NEC runs the risk of generating greater competi-*

tion and increased rivalry between the NSC and the NEC. That is why we have emphasized elsewhere in this report the importance of appointing individuals to White House positions who have compatible personalities and complementary skills.

- *Although the NEC should not be regarded as an entity subordinate to the NSC, it is the NSC that must attempt to provide a unified perspective on U.S. foreign policy. Thus, the NSC must take ultimate responsibility for preparing briefing papers, options memoranda, talking points, and other foreign policy materials for the president.*

Integrating Economics with Domestic Policy

- The NEC was given a mandate to handle microeconomic as well as macroeconomic issues, to address policy areas that previously would have been considered "domestic" rather than "economic," and, generally, to consider issues "importantly affecting the national economy."
- Not surprisingly, the administration and the NEC have implemented this sweeping mandate on an uneven basis.
- As noted above, the NEC structured its domestic staff assignments—and thus its institutional priorities—generally in accordance with the subject-matter areas specified in the January 1993 "charter" memorandum. Over the course of the Clinton administration, the NEC served as coordinator in developing a number of administration proposals and programs in these areas. Examples include:
  - A three-point program to increase private investment in economically distressed areas: creation of "empowerment zones" (enacted as part of the 1993 budget package); federal support for community development financial institutions (enacted in 1994); and reform of the Community Reinvestment Act (regulations finalized in 1995).
  - A defense base closures plan, designed to cushion the economic consequences that state and local economies suffer following base closings. The NEC coordinated the development of a strategy that stressed facilitating the private eco-

nomic development of these former base areas and actively monitored its implementation by the Department of Defense.

- An array of technology policy and research and development initiatives, including the Defense Reinvestment and Transition Initiative; expansion of the Advanced Technology Program in the Department of Commerce; increased funding for technology transfer work at the national laboratories, environmental technology, renewable energy, high-performance computing and communications, and "dual-use" research and development programs; and (jointly with the Office of Science and Technology Policy) establishment of an administration National Information Infrastructure (NII) Task Force.
- Initiatives for regulatory reform of financial institutions: interstate banking legislation (enacted in 1994), reduction of bank regulatory burdens (enacted in 1994), and reform of the bank and thrift insurance funds (enacted in 1996).
- Comprehensive Superfund reform, developed in a process cochaired by the Office of Environmental Policy and the NEC and designed to reduce litigation and transaction costs (introduced in Congress in 1994 but not passed).

- The NEC also handled issues that did not always fit neatly into its initially defined priority areas.
  - For example, the president asked the NEC to give him a proposal to respond to a report from the General Accounting Office documenting the poor physical condition of schools nationwide. The NEC coordinated a process that led to a proposal for the federal government to offer interest subsidies to state and local governments that modernize, renovate, and construct schools. This was enacted in 1996.
  - The NEC resolved a fractious dispute within the administration over whether to go forward with Export-Import Bank funding for the sale of U.S. engines and avionics for incorporation in new Russian civilian aircraft. This issue came to the NEC not because it was a presidential priority but because stalemate among the concerned agencies led them to seek a neutral White House broker to help resolve the matter.

- In addition, the NEC cochaired or otherwise participated in the process for developing and coordinating initiatives with other White House entities, principally the Domestic Policy Council (DPC). Examples include reforming the student loan program (led by the DPC), the school-to-work legislation (in conjunction with the DPC), and the consolidation of dozens of worker training programs into one program (OMB played a major role on this initiative).
- The NEC, however, was not effectively included in the development of some domestic initiatives with major economic effects.
    - On perhaps the two most significant domestic issues addressed by the Clinton administration, the 1994 health care reform proposal and welfare reform, virtually all of those interviewed felt that the NEC and its members were not effectively involved in the decisionmaking process.[7]
    - Although the NEC played a major role in the Superfund initiative noted above and participated in a limited number of other environmental matters, it does not appear to have contributed on a consistent basis to environmental policy development nor to regulatory policy outside the financial institutions area.
- The fact that the NEC was not consistently involved on all major domestic issues with significant economic dimensions appears to be attributable to several causes:
    - The NEC's mandate was extremely broad and, as a fledgling entity, the NEC probably needed to focus on selected "core" issues. In fact, the primary focus of the NEC advisor and the deputy advisors has been on establishing the credibility of the coordinating process, and, as a substantive matter, on budget policy and international trade policy.
    - Major figures in the White House do not appear to have been committed to the implications of the expansive rheto-

7. We understand that, since the failure of the 1994 health care proposal, the NEC has become much more actively involved in health care issues and that a key staff expert working on these issues reports to the leadership of both the DPC and the NEC (in a manner similar to the reporting of the international economics staff to both the NEC and the NSC).

ric in the NEC's charter, which gave it responsibility on *all* issues "importantly affecting the national economy."

- The overlap in jurisdiction between the NEC and the DPC raises the question whether the NEC is really needed to coordinate most domestic policy matters. In principle, as occurred in other administrations, many of these issues could be managed by a DPC rather than an NEC. However, a number of officials in the Clinton administration identified ways in which the NEC adds value to the process.
  - The presence of agencies and officials oriented toward economic issues results in questions being asked that might not otherwise be considered and imposes an economic discipline on social reform proposals that makes for better policy.
  - At a time when the efficacy of social programs is highly suspect in Congress and some elements of the private sector, generating more disciplined proposals can be politically advantageous, and gaining the support of the economic agencies may give such proposals added credibility.
  - The process of identifying and analyzing a traditional policy issue such as educational reform as an *economic* issue underscores the priority that the president seeks to attach to strengthening the economy.
- There does not now appear, however, to be a clear set of principles demarcating which issues lie within the NEC's jurisdiction and which are the province of other entities, such as the DPC, the Council on Environmental Quality, or the Office of the Vice President, nor which issues will be taken up for interagency coordination by the NEC and which will be left to individual agencies.
- In addition, it is not clear that the priorities initially reflected in recruiting NEC staff members and assigning responsibility to subject-matter clusters remain current.

RECOMMENDATION:
- *The new administration should ensure consistent NEC coordination and integration with the apparatus for domestic policy management, so that major issues with economic dimensions, such as entitlement reform, health care and welfare reform,*

environmental protection, and regulatory policy, receive mean-
ingful NEC attention.

- *The president and his key advisors can determine on a*
  case-by-case basis whether the NEC's role should be one
  of coordinator, joint coordinator, or participant in a pro-
  cess managed by another entity.
- *On the basis of decisions about the administration's stra-*
  tegic agenda and priorities and the NEC's role with re-
  spect to each of the priority issues, the NEC should make
  adjustments in the subject-matter areas covered by its staff.
- *Although it is beyond the scope of this report to make rec-*
  ommendations concerning the organization of White
  House domestic policy management, many officials with
  whom we spoke felt that NEC participation in domestic
  policymaking would probably be more effective if respon-
  sibility for coordinating domestic policy issues were more
  clearly demarcated than was the case during the first
  Clinton term.

Setting Strategic Priorities

- The NEC has not, to date, employed a systematic process for
  enabling the president and the administration to establish economic policy priorities, set goals, and assign responsibility for
  achieving them.
  - In its first year, the administration did use the NEC pro-
    cess—specifically, the NEC-led budget process—to deter-
    mine the initial wave of its domestic priorities. On the
    international side, the need to pass implementing legisla-
    tion for the NAFTA and the widespread concern about the
    trade deficit with Japan defined the administration's top
    economic policy priorities.
  - In its second year, the administration, independently of the
    NEC, defined comprehensive health care reform as its over-
    riding domestic priority.
  - In 1995 and 1996, the new Republican majority in Congress
    set the policy agenda, and the administration adopted a pos-
    ture of principally responding to congressional initiatives.

- The NEC has, however, taken some steps toward setting strategic priorities, especially in the area of international economic policy.
  - We understand that in 1996 NEC Advisor Laura Tyson initiated a series of principals meetings—some jointly with the NSC—to examine anticipated issues in particular subject-matter areas, such as U.S.-China relations, in an effort to sort out administration priorities and agency responsibilities.
  - The NEC also has provided an overall strategic focus for regional economic summits—APEC (for Asia), Summit of the Americas (for Latin America), and the Trans-Atlantic Agenda (for Europe)—and in shaping the U.S. position at the G-7 summits.
- The NEC is in a position to play a major role in defining the economic agenda for the new administration—if it acts quickly and effectively.

RECOMMENDATION:
- *Immediately after the election, the NEC should undertake a systematic process for setting strategic economic priorities and goals for the coming year.*
  - *The NEC, working with and drawing on the resources of other entities as appropriate, should have responsibility to identify major domestic and international economic issues, recommend presidential priorities, and provide a coherent framework for approaching these issues.*
  - *The process should produce well-defined goals and specific assignments of responsibility for achieving them.*
  - *The process of developing the next annual budget should be regarded as a related, but not equivalent, exercise.*
- *This exercise of setting of strategic economic priorities for the president should be repeated annually.*

- In addition to setting strategic priorities on an annual basis, the NEC also could perform an important function for the president in terms of longer-term thinking about the nation's economic performance.

- Long-term forecasts and goals recently have been incorporated in discrete public policy decisions—for example, the Clinton administration's initial five-year deficit reduction plan and the plan of the 104th Congress for phasing in a balanced budget in seven years.
- The entitlement reform challenges that will be high on the agenda of the president and the Congress over the next four years heavily depend on the accurate projection and interpretation of demographic trends.

- The NEC should take the lead in enabling the administration to move beyond incorporating long-term forecasts into policy on a case-by-case basis toward seeking to articulate on a systematic basis the major economic challenges in the years ahead and suggesting approaches for dealing with these challenges.

RECOMMENDATION: The NEC, again working with and drawing on the resources of others as appropriate, should ensure that the administration is aware of longer-term economic trends, both domestically and internationally, and considers alternative policy strategies and scenarios for addressing those trends.

Making the Process Work

Prerequisite 1: The Right Kind of Leadership—Gravitas with No Sharp Elbows

- An effective coordination process is one that, above all, is used—by the president and the relevant group of his advisors—as a more or less exclusive channel for communicating recommendations and making decisions on major policy issues. To run an entity in the White House that consistently plays this role requires a mix of qualities not frequently found in the same person:
    - Substantive ability and knowledge of the relevant policy area sufficient to command credibility among peers in the administration and in relevant external communities, which, for the NEC, include the Congress; U.S. and foreign financial, business, and labor circles; foreign governments; the media; and academia.

- Political judgment and process skills.
- Organizational leadership and management skills.
- A temperament that inspires both trust and confidence by reflecting the attributes of a true honest broker: the ability to solicit views from all sides, regardless of personal opinion, and to make clear that attempts to end-run the coordination process will not be tolerated.
- Finding individuals who fit this bill is a definite challenge, but one that a president must meet if he is to have an entity such as the NEC work well to serve his needs. The most successful White House policy coordinators—both Democratic and Republican—have displayed these qualities.

Prerequisite 2: Presidential Support for the Process

- If the president does not consistently use the policy coordination process for obtaining information, resolving disputes, and making decisions, no one will take it seriously. The president must demonstrate that the process serves his needs and must signal that end runs, leaks, or unilateral public pronouncements on policy will not be tolerated.
  - In the Ford administration, after Secretary of State Henry Kissinger gave a speech on a foreign economic policy issue without clearing it through the EPB, President Ford reportedly communicated his disappointment at a private luncheon meeting with Secretary Kissinger in the White House. According to those we interviewed, there were no recurrences.
  - At one point during a previous administration, a disgruntled cabinet member sought to end-run the interagency process by seeking an appointment with the president to contest an interagency group recommendation. The president, following the advice of the interagency group coordinator, both granted the appointment and made a decision even less favorable to the complaining cabinet member than the interagency group's original recommendation.
- President Clinton signaled his intention to make use of the NEC coordination process even before his inauguration when, at Rob-

ert Rubin's request, he hosted the six-hour meeting in Little Rock noted above.

- Subsequently, the president reinforced the message when he directly participated in the intensive NEC meetings that produced the February 1993 five-year deficit reduction plan.
- There have been some instances of NEC members acting outside the NEC process, such as Labor Secretary Reich's public support in early 1996 for tax incentive legislation to discourage corporate "downsizing," a concept strongly opposed by Treasury Secretary Rubin and NEC Advisor Tyson. We were told that Reich's campaign, which President Clinton appeared to tolerate for several weeks, finally ended when Chief of Staff Panetta met with Reich and either directed or persuaded him to cease such conduct.

Prerequisite 3: Agency Support for the Process

- Policy coordinators from several administrations stressed that, in order for agencies to support the coordination process, the agency players must perceive that their interests are served by working within the system, bringing issues to it, and preserving its integrity. To instill this perception, the coordinator must consistently grant cooperating agency heads a fair hearing and equal access to the president.
- Participant support for the NEC can be buttressed by the enhanced access and influence afforded to members through the coordination process. In particular, the CEA, originally thought to be diminished in stature by the creation of another senior economic position in the White House, gained "a seat at the table" on a more consistent basis because of the NEC.
- Agency heads perceive both pluses and minuses in bringing an agency initiative to the NEC: on the one hand, the initiative will be subjected to the potentially adverse judgment of other NEC members; on the other hand, if adopted by the NEC, the initiative will go forward with augmented support.
  - In 1996, the Department of Labor sought to revive consideration of administration support for a minimum wage bill, which President Clinton had previously rejected at the urg-

ing of economic team members other than Labor Secretary
Reich.
- Labor put the issue before the NEC, with a positive result.
  One NEC member stated that, without the face-to-face give
  and take afforded by the NEC environment, the administration probably would not have decided to push for enactment of a minimum wage bill in 1996.

Prerequisite 4: Regular, Frequent Contact among Members

- Many of those interviewed stressed the importance of frequent
  contact at the principals and deputies levels, including actual
  face-to-face meetings, in order for members to learn to work as
  a team.
  - Principals on the Executive Committee of the Ford EPB (who
    held roughly the same positions as the NEC "core mem-
    bers") met *daily* in the White House at 8:00 in the morning.
    (EPB Executive Director William Seidman circulated an
    agenda for each meeting to the entire cabinet the afternoon
    before, and every cabinet member was entitled to attend a
    particular meeting if a subject pertinent to his interests was
    scheduled for consideration.)
  - The Clinton NEC team appears to have "bonded" during
    the intensive meetings at which the 1993 budget plan was
    formulated. NEC deputies now meet weekly; principals meet
    irregularly but, we were told, frequently.
  - Clinton administration trade negotiators felt one benefit of
    their frequent meetings was that it became relatively easy
    to gain consensus on emergency conference calls during
    negotiating sessions when decisions had to be made imme-
    diately.

Prerequisite 5: The Right Balance among Flexibility, Formality, and Efficiency

- As a start-up entity with broad jurisdiction, the NEC had the
  potential to be seen by cabinet secretaries and their subordinates as infringing on their turf and their stature. On occasion,
  in previous administrations, there have been senior White House

advisors who have substantially diminished the role and authority of cabinet agencies. Noting this, many of those interviewed emphasized the conscious—and beneficial—decision made by Robert Rubin at the outset of the Clinton administration to conduct NEC affairs in a way that would not be perceived as threatening by cabinet secretaries. Agency confidence was initially fostered by:

- Designing meetings to be inclusive rather than exclusive, which sometimes led to very large attendance.
- Rarely establishing fixed or rigid agendas for meetings.
- Encouraging a freewheeling discussion.
- Refraining from assigning specific tasks to to one agency rather than another.

- This collegial approach was highly successful in building trust among the principals and their subordinates in a new White House entity and in the NEC process generally. According to one senior official: "It was important, particularly at the beginning, to allow for an open exchange, without bureaucratic constraint or clear jurisdictional lines, and for the participants to develop an understanding of their respective roles and trust in the coordination process."
- But cabinet secretaries and other senior U.S. government officials are busy people, with crowded schedules and limited time. Some of the drawbacks of the NEC's collegial style included:
  - Too many meetings.
  - Meetings that lasted too long.
  - Meetings that were without clear objectives and that did not produce decisions.
- One senior official, who is otherwise complimentary of the NEC, stated: "There were meetings which had no purpose, no endpoint, and at which decisions were never made." In the words of another official, "We had brainstorming sessions, rather than decision meetings."
- As the NEC evolves from its nascent stages to a more established coordinating body, it should be willing to sacrifice some of its flexibility in favor of greater formality and efficiency. Again, to quote a senior NEC member: "Now there is more confidence in the process and it is possible to streamline it and add some discipline to it."

- There are successful examples of more disciplined coordinating processes from other administrations. For example, members of the Ford administration highly praised William Seidman for running a "tight" meeting process, which included:
  - Creating a sharp distinction between "decision" meetings and "discussion" meetings. Decision meetings were the norm and were limited in size to representatives of only those agencies involved in the issue for decision and to only one or two representatives from each agency.
  - Circulating agendas and discussion papers in advance of decision meetings.
  - Limiting the duration of such meetings to one hour, so that cabinet secretaries could stick to crowded schedules.
  - Concluding meetings with a clear set of written instructions. (There also were minutes kept of meetings, though in this day of routine congressional requests for executive branch documents, it is understandable why an administration might be reluctant to keep complete minutes of internal meetings.)
  - Holding large "discussion" meetings less frequently—on a monthly or quarterly basis—in order to inform the full membership of major developments or initiatives and seek broad member input.
- Like William Seidman, Robert Gates, the deputy NSC advisor during the first part of the Bush administration, also is well known for running a disciplined meeting process. Gates always concluded meetings with a clear summing up of what had been decided and to whom certain tasks were delegated. "Perhaps Gates was a bit strict in his approach, but the meetings were crisp and the process worked well," said one participant in such meetings.
- The NEC has in fact begun to implement some of the steps that were so successful to the coordination processes of the Ford EPB and the Bush NSC. It should strive to do even more. Although the NEC currently has an executive secretary to assist in its management, the formal creation of a small secretariat could be a significant improvement.

RECOMMENDATION: The NEC should create a three-person secretariat, consisting of mid-level professionals, to ensure that agendas and discussion papers are provided well in advance of meetings of the deputies or principals, to circulate decision memoranda or written instructions to all relevant agencies subsequent to meetings, to assist the NEC staff in monitoring the implementation of tasks assigned to the agencies, and to enhance coordination with the NSC and its secretariat (as noted above).

Prerequisite 6: Effective Utilization of Staff

- The NEC's effectiveness depends, in part, on the composition of its staff, including the stature and authority of staff members, the mix of political appointees and civil servants, and the provision of support functions.
- *Stature and authority.* As in the case of the NEC advisor, the staff should possess a mix of skills and expertise. These include:
    - Being enough of a generalist to be knowledgeable about issues in a relevant substantive cluster.
    - Being enough of a specialist to know when agencies are distorting information, pushing parochial priorities, or otherwise skewing the process.
    - Being familiar and comfortable with the politics and processes of government, yet also having sufficient experience in the private sector to appreciate the real-world consequences of government decisions.
    - Being perceived as speaking and acting on behalf of the NEC advisor and thus possessing the authority (and guidance) to stimulate the interagency process as necessary, resolve interagency disputes when appropriate, yet avoid the temptation to usurp roles that can effectively be performed by the agencies.
- Many of those with whom we spoke perceive the NEC staff, especially on the domestic side, as in some cases lacking authority to serve as interagency coordinators and lacking in guidance from and the ability to speak for their superiors.

RECOMMENDATION:
- *There should be a greater delineation between senior and junior members of the NEC staff and more effective utilization of staff.*

- *The NEC advisor should appoint a small cadre of senior NEC staff (currently bearing the title "special assistant to the president for economic policy") who possess sufficient stature and are delegated sufficient authority to take a leadership role in harnessing agency expertise and resources to coordinate major economic issues facing the administration.*
- *This senior cadre should be supported by a sufficient number of staff members to perform the necessary coordination function. Although we believe that there should be a vertical structure to the NEC staff, we are not in a position to determine whether the current NEC staff size (approximately twenty professional members) is appropriate. The NEC advisor should not be constrained by this number if more (or fewer) staff are needed to perform the required work.*

- *Political versus career.* Political appointees and career civil servants each bring important, though different, qualities to government service.
  - Political appointees often are better attuned to the president's priorities, have valuable private-sector experience and contacts, and possess fresh energy and creativity.
  - Career civil servants often have great expertise and familiarity with the issues, understand how the agencies work, provide continuity and "institutional memory" from administration to administration, and are dedicated to public service.
  - The best organizations take maximum advantage of this mix of talents by utilizing good people from both groups.
- The NEC has made little use of career civil servants, and many White House officials expressed concern about doing so. While recognizing that the NSC staff includes many career employees, the NEC members who expressed such concern felt that domestic issues tend to be more inherently political in nature than the issues handled by the NSC.
- Ironically, however, a number of the senior political figures with whom we spoke (who had served in government for extended

periods of time at the highest levels) unanimously praised the virtues of career civil servants. Moreover, they noted that, in their view, it is political appointees, not civil servants, who usually leak sensitive information to the media.

RECOMMENDATION: The NEC would benefit from the detailing of career employees from departments such as Treasury, Commerce, and perhaps others. These individuals can strengthen and help institutionalize the NEC over time, by adding continuity and "memory" to NEC activities. The NEC advisor also should consider staffing the NEC secretariat with civil servants.

- *Support functions.* Some coordinating bodies, such as the NSC, have their own legal counsel, legislative liaison, and press officer. The NEC does not have these support personnel directly within the organization; it relies instead on White House support functions.
- There are a variety of reasons why the NSC has developed these internal support functions, including the need for "top secret" security clearances for NSC matters, the crisis (time-sensitive) nature of many NSC issues, and concern about activities of former NSC staff members who allegedly violated the law.
- Although some of those interviewed questioned whether the NSC truly needed these support functions (as opposed to relying on White House functions), virtually everyone we interviewed felt that the NEC's activities did not require the addition of these support functions to its staff.

RECOMMENDATION: The NEC should resist creating additional support positions beyond a secretariat. The NEC has a fluid agenda cutting across a wide range of issues and agencies; it should work directly with existing White House support functions.

Prerequisite 7: Effective Relations with the Agencies

- The NEC has provided an effective forum for White House decisions by cabinet and subcabinet officers. It does not appear, however, that the NEC has always made maximum use of its member agencies at the working level. There was general criticism among those with whom we spoke that issues have often been elevated to the NEC deputies and principals too quickly.

- The quick elevation of issues precluded preparatory work by the agencies before discussion by the NEC deputies.
- The quick elevation of issues also may have created at times a gulf between those who are making decisions in the White House and those who must implement them in the bureaucracy.
- The NEC should not serve as a substitute for interagency deliberations, where the relevant agencies often can work through the issues and resolve disagreements. Where they are unable to resolve their differences, the agencies can provide their views on the policy trade-offs in briefing memoranda for the political-level decisionmakers.
- The NEC's strengths are in identifying major economic policy issues and ensuring the incorporation of those issues into the executive branch policymaking process; mobilizing information and analysis; monitoring interagency consideration of issues; resolving disagreements when possible; and, if necessary, assisting in the clarification of major policy options that emerge from the interagency machinery.

RECOMMENDATION; The NEC staff should monitor, stimulate, and intervene when necessary in interagency processes to resolve issues without elevating them to higher levels; should inform their superiors (and through them the president) of ongoing decision processes and likely results if the president does not intervene (to give him a chance to do so); and, when issues are elevated, should oversee the preparation of discussion papers for consideration by the NEC deputies and principals (or other channels to the president).

The Question of Codification of the NEC by Statute

- Each modern administration has utilized one or more mechanisms for coordinating economic policy. However, unlike the NSC, which by statute has provided institutional continuity in the national security area for almost fifty years, none of the White House–based coordinating mechanisms dedicated to economic policy has endured over time; they have often disappeared with the change of administration.

- The NEC represents a significant first step by the Clinton administration toward establishing a substantial White House entity to enhance the coordination of economic policymaking and increase the impact of economic considerations in policy decisions.

- Even the most ardent supporters of the NEC with whom we spoke, however, stated that the president should retain the flexibility to organize his administration—and, in particular, the operations of the White House—in a manner that is most compatible with his personal style and policy objectives.

- We believe—-and virtually all of those interviewed concurred— that the next step in the evolution of the NEC is to strengthen and institutionalize the organization and its processes without trying to freeze the NEC structure in statute.

RECOMMENDATION: It is premature to seek to codify the NEC structure by statute, and we recommend against such a step.

Appendix 1
Executive Order 12835

Establishment of the National Economic Council

January 25, 1993

By the authority vested in me as President of the United States by the Constitution and the laws of the United States of America, including sections 105, 107, and 301 of title 3, United States Code, it is hereby ordered as follows:

Section 1. Establishment. There is established the National Economic Council ("the Council").

Sec. 2. Membership. The Council shall comprise the:
    (a) President, who shall serve as Chairman of the Council;
    (b) Vice President;
    (c) Secretary of State;
    (d) Secretary of the Treasury;
    (e) Secretary of Agriculture;
    (f) Secretary of Commerce;
    (g) Secretary of Labor;
    (h) Secretary of Housing and Urban Development;
    (i) Secretary of Transportation;
    (j) Secretary of Energy;

(k) Administrator of the Environmental Protection Agency;

(l) Chair of the Council of Economic Advisers;

(m) Director of the Office of Management and Budget;

(n) United States Trade Representative;

(o) Assistant to the President for Economic Policy;

(p) Assistant to the President for Domestic Policy;

(q) National Security Adviser;

(r) Assistant to the President for Science and Technology Policy; and

(s) Such other officials of executive departments and agencies as the President may, from time to time, designate.

Sec. 3. Meetings of the Council. The President, or upon his direction, the Assistant to the President for Economic Policy ("the Assistant"), may convene meetings of the Council. The President shall preside over the meetings of the Council, provided that in his absence the Vice President, and in his absence the Assistant, will preside.

Sec. 4. Functions. (a) The principal functions of the Council are: (1) to coordinate the economic policy-making process with respect to domestic and international economic issues; (2) to coordinate economic policy advice to the President; (3) to ensure that economic policy decisions and programs are consistent with the President's stated goals, and to ensure that those goals are being effectively pursued; and (4) to monitor implementation of the President's economic policy agenda. The Assistant may take such actions, including drafting a Charter, as may be necessary or appropriate to implement such functions.

(b) All executive departments and agencies, whether or not represented on the Council, shall coordinate economic policy through the Council.

(c) In performing the foregoing functions, the Assistant will, when appropriate, work in conjunction with the Assistant to the President for Domestic Policy and the Assistant to the President for National Security.

(d) The Secretary of the Treasury will continue to be the senior economic official in the executive branch and the President's chief economic spokesperson. The Director of the Office of Management and Budget, as the President's principal budget spokesperson, will continue to be the senior budget official in the executive branch. The Council of Economic Advisers will continue its traditional analytic, forecasting and advisory functions.

Sec. 5. Administration. (a) The Council may function through established or ad hoc committees, task forces or interagency groups.

(b) The Council shall have a staff to be headed by the Assistant to the President for Economic Policy. The Council shall have such staff and other assistance as may be necessary to carry out the provisions of this order.

(c) All executive departments and agencies shall cooperate with the Council and provide such assistance, information, and advice to the Council as the Council may request, to the extent permitted by law.

WILLIAM CLINTON
THE WHITE HOUSE,
January 25, 1993

Appendix 2
Presidential Decision Directive/NEC-2

The White House, Washington
March 24, 1993

TO: THE VICE PRESIDENT
      THE SECRETARY OF STATE
      THE SECRETARY OF THE TREASURY
      THE SECRETARY OF AGRICULTURE
      THE SECRETARY OF COMMERCE
      THE SECRETARY OF LABOR
      THE SECRETARY OF HOUSING AND URBAN DEVELOPMENT
      THE SECRETARY OF TRANSPORTATION
      THE SECRETARY OF ENERGY
      THE ADMINISTRATOR OF THE ENVIRONMENTAL PROTECTION AGENCY
      THE CHAIR OF THE COUNCIL OF ECONOMIC ADVISERS
      THE DIRECTOR OF THE OFFICE OF MANAGEMENT AND BUDGET
      THE UNITED STATES TRADE REPRESENTATIVE
      THE ASSISTANT TO THE PRESIDENT FOR ECONOMIC POLICY
      THE ASSISTANT TO THE PRESIDENT FOR DOMESTIC POLICY
      THE NATIONAL SECURITY ADVISER
      THE ASSISTANT TO THE PRESIDENT FOR SCIENCE AND TECHNOLOGY
        POLICY

SUBJECT: Organization of the National Economic Council

To assist me in carrying out my responsibilities in the area of the national economy, I hereby direct that the National Economic Council system be organized as follows.

A. The National Economic Council (NEC)

The National Economic Council will be the principal forum for consideration of economic policy issues requiring Presidential determination. The responsibility, functions, and membership of the NEC shall be as set forth in Executive Order 12835 and this Presidential Decision Directive. The NEC shall (1) advise and assist me in integrating all aspects of national economic policy—macro-economics, micro-economics, domestic, international and sectoral (in conjunction with the National Security Council); (2) develop and manage the economic policy-making processes with respect to domestic and international economic issues; (3) coordinate economic policy advice to the President; (4) ensure that economic policy decisions and programs are consistent with the President's stated goals, and ensure that those goals are being effectively pursued; and (5) monitor implementation of the President's economic policy agenda. The Assistant to the President for Economic Policy may take such actions as may be necessary or appropriate to implement these responsibilities. As provided in Executive Order 12835, (1) the Council may function through established or ad hoc committees, task forces or interagency groups. (2) The Council shall have a staff to be headed by the Assistant to the President for Economic Policy. The Council shall have such a staff and other assistance as may be necessary to carry out the provisions of this order. (3) All executive departments and agencies shall cooperate with the Council and provide such assistance, information, and advice to the Council as the Council may request, to the extent permitted by law. Along with its subordinate committees, the NEC shall be my principal means for coordinating Executive departments and agencies in the development and implementation of national security [*sic*] policy.

The NEC shall have as its members the President, the Vice President, the Secretary of State, the Secretary of the Treasury, the Secretary of Agriculture, the Secretary of Commerce, the Secretary of Labor, the Secretary of Housing and Urban Development, the Secretary of Transportation, the Secretary of Energy, the Administrator of the Environmental Protection Agency, the Chair of the Council of Economic Advisers, the Director of the Office of Management and Budget, the United States Trade Representative, the Assistant to the President for Economic Policy, the Assistant to the President for Domestic Policy, the National Security Adviser, and the Assistant to the President for Science and Technology Policy. The heads of other Executive departments and agencies and other senior officials shall be invited to attend meetings of the NEC where appropriate.

The NEC shall meet as required. The Assistant to the President for Economic Policy, at my direction and, when appropriate, in consultation with the Secretary of the Treasury, the Director of the OMB, and the Assistant to the President for National Security Affairs, shall be responsible for determining the agenda and ensuring that the necessary papers are prepared. Other members of the NEC may propose items for inclusion on the agenda. The Assistant to the President shall be assisted by a National Economic Council staff.

B. The NEC Principals Committee (ECON1)

An NEC Principals Committee is established as the senior interagency forum for the consideration and integration of policy issues importantly affecting the national economy. The NEC Principals Committee shall review, coordinate, and monitor the development and implementation of national economic policy. The NEC/PC should be a flexible instrument—a forum available for Cabinet-level officials to meet to discuss and resolve issues not requiring the President's participation. The Assistant to the President for Economic Policy will serve as chair of the NEC Principals Committee. The Assistant to the President for National Security Affairs shall be informed of meetings and invited to attend all those with international economic and international security implications and considerations.

The NEC Principals Committee shall have as its members the Secretary of the Treasury; the Director of the Office of Management and Budget; the Chairman of the Council of Economic Advisers; the Secretary of Commerce; and the Secretary of Labor; and the Assistant to the President for National Security Affairs as appropriate. Other heads of departments or agencies shall be invited as needed.

The Assistant to the President for National Economic Policy shall be responsible—in consultation with the Secretary of Treasury and the Director of OMB, and, when appropriate, the Assistant to the President for National Security Affairs—for calling meetings of the NEC/PC, for determining the agenda, and for ensuring that the necessary papers are prepared.

C. The NEC Deputies Committee (ECON2)

An NEC Deputies Committee shall serve as the senior sub-Cabinet interagency forum for consideration of policy issues affecting the national economy. The NEC Deputies Committee shall review and monitor the work of the NEC interagency process (including Interagency Working Groups established pursuant to Section D below). The Deputies Committee also shall focus significant attention on policy implementation. Periodic reviews of the Administration's major economic initiatives shall be scheduled to ensure that they are being implemented in a timely and effective manner. Also, these reviews should periodically consider whether existing policy directives should be revamped or rescinded.

The NEC Deputies Committee shall have as its members the Deputy Assistant to the President for Economic Policy (who will serve as the chairman) and the appropriate senior officials of Deputy Secretary or Under Secretary rank chosen by the relevant heads of departments or agencies which compose the NEC in consultation with the Deputy Assistant to the President for Economic Policy. The Deputy Assistant to the President for National Security Affairs shall be a member of the NEC Deputies Committee and attend meetings as needed. The Deputy Assistant to the President for Economic Policy may invite representatives of other Executive departments and agencies, and other senior officials, to attend meetings of the NEC Deputies Committee where appropriate in light of the issues to be discussed.

The Deputy Assistant to the President for Economic Policy shall be responsible for calling meetings of the NEC Deputies Committee, for determining the agenda, and for ensuring that the necessary papers are prepared. The NEC Deputies Committee shall ensure that all papers to be discussed by the NEC or the NEC Principals Committee fully analyze the issues, fairly and adequately set out the facts, consider full range of views and options, and satisfactorily assess the prospects, risks, and implications of each. The NEC Deputies Committee may task the interagency groups established pursuant to Section D of this Presidential Decision Directive.

D. Interagency Working Groups (ECON3)

A system of Interagency Working Groups—some permanent, others *ad hoc*—is hereby authorized. The NEC Interagency Working Groups shall be established at the direction of the Deputies Committee, which shall also determine the chair of the NEC Interagency Working Groups—either departmental or NSC, NEC, or DPC. The Interagency Working Groups shall convene on a regular basis—to be determined by the Deputies Committee—to review and coordinate in the implementation of Presidential decisions in their policy areas. Strict guidelines shall be established governing the operation of the Interagency Working Groups, including participants, decision-making path and time frame. The number of these working groups shall be kept to the minimum needed to promote an effective NEC system.

WILLIAM J. CLINTON